MW00789920

MOTHER ANGELICA'S
QUICK GUIDE TO THE SACRAMENTS

Also by Mother Angelica:

Praying with Mother Angelica
Meditations on the Rosary,
the Way of the Cross,
and Other Prayers

Mother Angelica's
Answers, Not Promises

Mother Angelica on
Christ and Our Lady

Mother Angelica on
Suffering and Burnout

MOTHER ANGELICA'S
QUICK GUIDE
TO THE
SACRAMENTS

EWTN PUBLISHING, INC.
Irondale, Alabama

Mother Angelica's Quick Guide to the Sacraments was originally published as eleven mini-books: *I Am His Temple* (1977), *My Encounter with Jesus through the Holy Spirit* (1976), *My Life in the Sacraments* (1976), *My Mother—The Church* (1976), *Sentinels Before the Bread of Life* (1976), *Struggle of a Soul's Purification* (1976), *Sweeping the Temple Clean* (1976), *The Living Sacrament—Matrimony* (1976), *The Mass in My Life* (1976), *To Leave and yet to Stay* (1977), and *Why Do You Stay Away?* (1976), copyright Our Lady of the Angels Monastery 3222 County Road 548, Hanceville, Alabama 35077, olamshrine.com, and printed with the ecclesiastical approval of Joseph G. Vath, D.D., Bishop of Birmingham, Alabama, USA.

Cover and interior design by Perceptions Design Studio.

Cover art: detail from official portrait by John Howard Sanden.

All quotations from Holy Scripture are taken from Jerusalem Bible, © 1966 by Darton Longman and Todd Ltd. and Doubleday and Company Ltd.

EWTN Publishing, Inc.
5817 Old Leeds Road, Irondale, AL 35210

Distributed by Sophia Institute Press, Box 5284, Manchester, NH 03108.

Library of Congress Cataloging-in-Publication Data
Names: M. Angelica (Mary Angelica), Mother, 1923-2016, author.
Title: Mother Angelica's quick guide to the sacraments.
Description: Irondale, Alabama : EWTN Publishing, Inc., 2017.
Identifiers: LCCN 2017013527 | ISBN 9781682780060 (hardcover : alk. paper)
Subjects: LCSH: Sacraments—Catholic Church.
Classification: LCC BX2200 .M122 2017 | DDC 234/.16—dc23 LC record available at https://lccn.loc.gov/2017013527

First printing

CONTENTS

Editor's Note

This volume brings together for the first time *I Am His Temple*, *My Encounter with Jesus through the Holy Spirit*, *My Life in the Sacraments*, *My Mother — The Church*, *Sentinels Before the Bread of Life*, *Struggle of a Soul's Purification*, *Sweeping the Temple Clean*, *The Living Sacrament — Matrimony*, *The Mass in My Life*, *To Leave and yet to Stay*, and *Why Do You Stay Away?*, eleven "mini-books" written by Mother Angelica and published by Our Lady of the Angels Monastery in the 1970s. Each section of this book corresponds to one of Mother's original mini-books. Taken together, they form a unique and beautiful work of spiritual wisdom and prayerful reverence.

Mother Angelica wrote these words on a pad of paper while in Adoration of the Blessed Sacrament in the chapel of her monastery in Irondale, Alabama. Her order, the Poor Clares of Perpetual Adoration, has been dedicated to the Blessed Sacrament since its founding, and so it is only fitting that Mother's written works were completed in His Presence.

By the mid-1970s, the Nuns of Our Lady of the Angels Monastery were printing as many as twenty-five thousand copies of these mini-books and others per day. This was truly a nascent mass-media operation, one that would lead to the creation of EWTN—the Eternal Word Television Network.

This book is a faithful representation of Mother Angelica's original work, with only the most basic corrections of printing errors, adjustments to formatting, and so on. You can be confident that you are reading an authentic presentation of the wisdom and spirituality of one of the most important figures in the history of Catholicism in America.

MOTHER ANGELICA'S
QUICK GUIDE TO
THE SACRAMENTS

My Life in the Sacraments

Baptism — Sacrament of Sonship

God is my Father! How can I fathom such a privilege? One moment I was a creature of an all-powerful God, and then suddenly the Sacrament of Baptism raised me to a dignity I cannot even imagine.

Before Creation, God chose me to be and then He chose me again to be His own Child. His love drew me to Himself by adopting me as His son. To make that sonship real and not imaginary He took up His dwelling in my soul. God — Father, Son, and Holy Spirit — lives in me. Why doesn't this reality possess my mind and move my heart to love Him more? Perhaps my difficulty lies in the enormity of this truth. Is it too great a mystery for my small mind to fathom? I fear I must admit it is the obligations of such a reality that make me tuck this truth away behind more mundane things where it is buried out of sight.

I am in His Presence everywhere I go. I should give Him to everyone I meet by being a son in deed and word. My attitude towards my neighbor should be one of love, humility, and goodness. Those attributes of God, my Father, must radiate in me so all men recognize Jesus in me. By Baptism I inherit His very own qualities, so I must be careful that no trial makes me anxious, no privation makes me worry, no pain makes me despair, no demands make me selfish, for I am a son of God—the same God whose providence takes care of the grass that fades and the birds that fall from the air—the same God who chose me from among millions of possible human beings to know and love Him—the same God who watches over me as if I were the only creature of His Hands. Today I will think often of my sonship—His Love for me, and how I must radiate that love to my neighbor.

Confession — Sacrament of Reconciliation

Sin is a weapon that wounds God, my neighbor, and myself. I cannot allow the realization that I cannot hurt God in His person, cloud the reality that whatever I do to my neighbor I do to Him. His Will has ordained that whatever evil or good I do—He is the recipient. "Why do you persecute Me?" He asked Paul (Acts 9:4). "I was hungry and you gave Me to eat," He told His Apostles (see Matt. 25:35).

Because I am His Temple, sin defiles this temple, for my will chooses self over God—for a moment the temple becomes totally mine and God is asked to leave. I prefer myself to Him—I prefer my own good to my neighbor's good.

When Jesus gave me the parable of the Prodigal Son He gave me an example of this triple effect of sin. The wayward son offended his father by disobedience; he offended society by his bad example; and he offended himself by becoming unworthy to eat even the food of pigs.

His humble repentance moved him to return first to his father and seek forgiveness, and then it was he began to repair the damage done to society. His humble repentance gave others a sense of goodness in mercy. His father's forgiveness restored his dignity as a son. His conversion from evil gave society the good example it so badly needed. The prodigal knew of his father's goodness while he was still in exile, but his human nature needed to hear the words of forgiveness with his own ears—he needed human assurance.

MOTHER ANGELICA'S QUICK GUIDE TO THE SACRAMENTS

I too have this need. The Father has given me the opportunity of hearing words of merciful love and feeling the burden of sin lift from my soul. Jesus presents Himself in the person of the priest to absolve me from my sins, heal my weaknesses, and restore my friendship with the Father. In reconciling myself with God, I am ready to love my neighbor with a deeper love and with unselfish motives.

Attitudes and motives that so often lead me to choose myself rather than God are laid bare, and I am better able to change my life. When I realize the areas of my soul in most need, I can direct my will to change so the image of Jesus in me grows brighter and brighter.

I thank You, Lord God, for the Sacrament that restores my friendship with You, purifies my attitudes, redirects my path, heals my weaknesses, and reconciles me to my neighbor.

Eucharist — Sacrament of Growth

It is beyond my comprehension to imagine God becoming man! I cannot understand such love for me. I am accustomed to limited love, and I find myself at a loss before the sight of Unlimited Love. Why am I in such a quandary? At least He had a human nature—a God-man, someone who ate, drank, slept, worked, spoke, and suffered.

It would seem that His love had reached its limits for God to lower Himself to such depths—but no—His love contrived a means by which He could come down to earth, redeem mankind, return triumphant to His Father, and yet stay with me during my earthly journey.

He would lower Himself to even greater depths of humility and obedience. He would continue to give me a living example of patience, love, and humility—He would be my solace in distress, my confidant in sorrow, my food for the journey, my grace to change, my joy in success, and my comfort in failure.

He gives me an example of obedience, for He comes down in the form of bread at the command of His priests. He stays in the tabernacle day after day, month after month, year after year, just so I may go to Him with my joys and sorrows. He humbles Himself and becomes my food so His own Body and Blood may course through my veins and I may be able to grow into His Image and please the Father.

He assured me that without Him I could do nothing, and it is His Presence in me that gives me eternal life. It is like Heaven all the way to Heaven.

Holy Communion permits me to share in His virtues so when the occasion to be virtuous arises, I possess within my very soul all the invisible qualities I need to bear fruit. My neighbor must see the results of every Communion by its effect in my daily life.

I must remember that through the frequent reception of this Sacrament, love and grace grow together in my soul. Through frequent visits to Jesus in the tabernacle, the spirit of prayer brings peace to my soul and through the power of the Eucharist in my Church and in my soul, the whole world is blessed, the enemy vanquished, and all mankind benefited.

Confirmation — Sacrament of Mission

When the Father called me out of nothingness He gave me life — when I was Baptized, He gave me sonship, but in Confirmation He gave me a mission — a purpose — a work to accomplish. This was the day of the Gift of Talents — talents I am expected to use, trade with, and increase.

Baptism gave me ten talents — Faith, Hope, Love, Fear of the Lord, Piety, Fortitude, Counsel, Knowledge, Understanding, and Wisdom. Throughout the years Baptism gave me a new dignity, Confession restored my friendship with God and neighbor, and Communion nourished my soul, making it grow strong in the Lord.

My life was a constant growing process of these three Sacraments, and as I reached a kind of spiritual teenage, Confirmation put upon my soul the finishing touch to everything I needed to bear fruit.

It was the day God said to me, "Go out and trade until I come." These four Sacraments must bear such great fruit in my soul that all men will know by my word and example that "Jesus is Lord" and that He loves them as much as the Father loves Him (John 17:23).

These ten talents must grow, increase, and multiply, and I should never forget I must render an account for them to the Lord of all, when His wisdom calls me home. Has Faith grown so I see God in every facet of my life? Do I grow in Hope when discouragement and sadness overtake me? Am I able to love first, always, and when I am not loved in return? Am I growing more sensitive to sin and sinful occasions because I do not wish to offend so loving a Father? Is every human being a brother in my heart? When temptation assails me or pain lingers on and on, do I have the courage to live through it and overcome? Can

I discern God's Will in my life when selfishness or the Enemy tries to dissuade me from the right choices?

Is my heart engrossed in spiritual realities or visible possessions? Can I perceive the Voice of the Spirit as He inspires me in Scripture and speaks to my soul? Is God's Presence around me and within me the source of my joy?

The answers to these questions will tell me whether I am growing and trading well with my ten talents. God forbid that when He comes He finds I have buried them all.

Matrimony — Sacrament of Union

Every Sacrament is an encounter with Jesus through the Holy Spirit—each one *is* a channel of grace—a visible sign of an invisible reality. I should look upon the Sacrament of Matrimony, not only as the union of two people into one, a union whose love cooperates with God in the continual creation of man, but as an image of the Trinity on earth. Every married couple and the children who proceed from that union should also remind me of the union of Christ with the Church, the union of Jesus with the soul, and the union of the members of the Mystical Body with Jesus, their Head.

In our family life, man represents the Eternal Father, and like the Father he is to be compassionate, merciful, provident, wise, protective, creative, and good; woman, who was taken from man, as Scripture tells us, represents Jesus in the family circle. Like Jesus she is to be a bond of reconciliation, gentle, loving, intuitive, sensitive to the needs of others, humble, and an example of patient suffering. Children represent the Spirit, for as the Spirit proceeds from Father and Son, so children proceed from father and mother.

They, like the Spirit, are a power that generates love, joy, and peace. They are to be obedient, thoughtful, considerate, helpful, and ever work toward unity among one another.

This earthly image of the Trinity that we call family life is not an unrealistic goal, but the obligation of every Christian family. Cities and nations are as strong as the families that live within them and the Christian family is God's message to the world. The message of peace and love are not spread by lovely individuals, but by members of families whose love for God has taught them how people of varying temperaments can live together in peace.

As the members of a family strive to grow in the position they hold in their family life, the whole Body of Christ grows stronger, the Church's Witnessing role is more powerful, and mankind is guided in the right path.

The home that has the Father as its Lord, Jesus as its Image, and the Spirit as its Guide possesses love, and that kind of love will change the world.

Holy Orders — Sacrament of Priesthood

Although Confirmation has made me a member of a priestly family in which I offer Jesus to the Father at every Mass, I should look at the Sacrament of Priesthood as it is given to those chosen sons of God—the ordained priests. How does his personal gift from God affect my daily life?

Little thought is necessary before I realize that without this Sacrament my daily life would be in darkness. It is the Priest whose consecrated hands bring down Jesus from Heaven. His words and power make ordinary bread and wine the Body and Blood of Christ. When I fall into sin, his hands are raised in absolution and the Mercy of God covers me like a mantle. He pours water over my head and makes me a child of God, anoints my head with chrism, and brings down the Spirit to fill me with Gifts.

He anoints my sick body with oil and brings upon me the healing power of Jesus. He discerns for me in matters of Faith and Morals and teaches me the way to God. He makes my parents one flesh, and as they grow old, he comforts them in their sorrows and prepares their souls for the journey home.

The question then is not how the Priest affects my life, but how I affect his. Am I loyal to him even when I see him imperfect? Do I forgive him his transgressions as he forgives mine? Do I extend my hand when he falls as his hand extends to me?

Am I critical over the splinter in his eye, when week after week I confess to him the beam in my own? Do I defend him before his enemies and overlook his defects? Am I willing to sacrifice my time for his sake as he does for mine? Do I ever thank him for his hard work and praise him for a job well done? Do I pray for him daily and ask God to make him holy?

Perhaps if I treated him with loving respect, gentle understanding, grateful praise, and brotherly forbearance, his life would be less lonely, his apostolate more fruitful, and his spiritual life more at peace. We must help each other as we faithfully follow the mission God has given to each of us.

Anointing — Sacrament of Healing

God pursues my soul throughout my life. When I am ill His Priest prays for my healing and places oil upon my brow as a sign of God's protection and care. He knew my soul would be at peace when I had a visible sign of His personal love. His loving providence designed that inner healing and renewed strength be mine even when my illness continued.

Jesus suffered from all the trials, pain, disappointments, and daily cares that are my portion. He realized from personal experience that death and its accompanying suffering would fill me with fears of the unknown.

To take away these fears He told me of Heaven and the specific place He would prepare for me. To comfort me He sends His Priest to anoint my body to obtain strength for the journey and absolve me from sin so my garments are pure white. He gives Himself to me in Holy Communion in order to be my companion from this life to the next. He promises me that angels will be with me and His own Mother will intercede for me.

This Sacrament is so powerful that if the Bridegroom should say, "Come" to me and I have given all things into His Hands and accepted death as His Holy Will with perfect peace, He and I shall go together to meet the Father face-to-face. This Sacrament will have placed the last jewel on my crown, the last pearl on my garment, the last ring on my finger, the last act of love that makes eternal life more glorious and my Vision of God more resplendent.

To the very last He draws good out of everything for my sake. His judgment will be merciful, His Love forever mine, His joy continually filling my soul to overflowing, and His knowledge enlightening my mind. Eternal Light will envelop a tiny spark, and at last we will be joined together as one Light — eternally.

My Mother — The Church

The word "Church" means many things to many people. To some the Church is merely a structure, a body of laws designed to make everyone as miserable as possible, an authoritarian body which takes delight in exercising the prerogative of telling the world what it can and cannot do.

There are others who look upon the Church as a vehicle through which God reveals Himself, His truths, and His Will. Others look upon it as the "opium of the people" or an organization that is guided by the will and whims of its members. Some look upon the Church as the embodiment of the arts and treasures of past ages — a kind of giant museum, rich in tradition and historical data, rich in material wealth but frugal in the distribution of that wealth.

Still others see the Church as a political power, able to influence the destinies of nations. Conservatives see the Church as the epitome of sound doctrine and dogma, while liberals see it as a source of sustenance for the poor, justice for the downtrodden, and a defense of the helpless. Fervent souls look upon the Church as a dispenser of grace through a sacramental system. Lukewarm souls have a half-hearted confidence in the realization that the Church will always be there when and if they need it. Souls who have chosen evil sometimes are more knowledgeable as to the true role of the Church and for that reason hate everything it stands for.

We could go on and on as to what the opinions and feelings of people are towards the Church. We could look at various theological aspects of its teaching authority and its apostolic succession, but we would inevitably reach an impasse with argument piled upon argument. With this in mind let us look at the Church and its function as St. Paul did and see it for what it is — the Bride of Christ, the Mother from whose womb of grace each of us was born to a new life, a life of Sonship.

Jesus lived, died, and rose to give birth to the Church. Through the Spirit He wed Her to Himself, perpetuates His Presence through Her sacraments, generates holy souls, raises those dead in sin to life, and continually feeds His children with the truth.

God created us to His Image, and that image is not only in the individual soul, but in the Church. Just as there are Three Persons in one God, three faculties in each soul, three elements to each family, so it is in the Church. The Church is the Dispenser of the Father's truth. It is the Bride of Jesus and is guided by His Spirit.

As the Holy Spirit proceeds from the love of the Father and the Son in the Trinity, as children brought forth from the love of husband and wife, so the Church, this gift of the Father, wedded to His Son, constantly brings forth the fruit of holiness through the power of the Spirit in all Her children.

The Word became Incarnate in the womb of Mary through the power of the Holy Spirit. This Divine Mystery is constantly reenacted as the Eternal Word is mirrored more and more perfectly in the Bride of Christ as She gives Jesus to Her children in the Eucharist, heals their wounds in Confession, ennobles their love through the Sacrament of Marriage, makes mere men priests of God through Ordination and sons of God in Baptism, enriches them with gifts in Confirmation, and then lightens their burden on their journey home through Anointing.

The Church is a Mother because She is a Bride who is forever bringing forth children of light, pillars of holiness, sources of inspiration, challengers of truth, and defenders of the Faith.

Yes, She has structures, laws, treasures, authority, and human frailties mixed with Divine power, but we must look at the whole Church and not just part of Her. What son of an earthly mother tells his friends that his mother is nothing but an ugly skeleton covered over with muscle and skin? What kind of son picks apart every fault and weakness in his mother and broadcasts it to everyone willing to listen? A child who concentrates only on the authority a mother has to correct and punish, and refuses to see the deep love and concern behind the reproaches, leads an unbalanced existence—a life of self-pity and childish peeves.

It is difficult to understand a child who criticizes the art treasures of his parents while partaking of the beauty of those treasures whenever he pleases. This would be especially true if those treasures were available for the poorest of the poor to see and enjoy. Would he be happier if all the treasures in the Church were sold to private collectors and hidden forever from the eyes of the poor? It is amazing how our human nature manages to concoct such tailor-made excuses to cover our antipathies for the Church. Many children hate their parents because they are corrected and directed by them, and so it is with Holy Mother Church. When She speaks about the necessity for high morals, deep faith, and self-control, human nature rebels, and She becomes the mean stepmother, the domineering parent, the epitome of archaic ideals. Then it is that foolproof reasons are created to explain their rebellion and make them feel justified. The garments of love, loyalty, and humility are replaced with the hard steel of pride and the acid ice of arrogance. No gentle persuasion can penetrate this coat of steel, for these misguided people mistake themselves for knights in shining armor, championing the cause of the misunderstood and misrepresented.

A true child of this God-given Mother is not one who is blind to Her faults, weaknesses, and wounds, but one who is discerning enough to see Her need for improvement, for healing, for greater zeal, and for generosity; loving enough to see Her virtues, grace, truth, and power; and zealous enough to do something positive to help rather than something negative to destroy.

We pride ourselves on building up those in despair, feeding the hungry, clothing the naked, and giving a cup of cold water to the thirsty. Why do we not render these same services to the Church? Does She not desire that Her children thirst for the living water of holiness? Does She not look for Her children to bear the fruits of the Spirit? Does She not feel the nakedness of Her children as they are despoiled of Faith, Hope, and Love by the spirit of this world? Does She not longingly wait for those who have left to return to the Father's house? Is Her heart not broken as She sees so many of Her children exposing their souls to the danger of Hell? What anguish tears at her heart as so many refuse the healing balm of Confession or the angelic food of the Eucharist?

What madness possesses our minds and souls, blinds our senses, and hardens our hearts towards so good a Mother? We pride ourselves on our maturity, freedom, and intelligence and then proceed to act like spoiled children who have been refused the privilege of playing with fire. We use our souls and our future like a game of Russian Roulette—pulling every trigger of presumption, pride, and arrogance to see what happens! Unfortunately, like those who play the game, there is no turning back if one loses.

"So I now say to you: you are Peter and on this rock I will build my Church" (Matt. 16:18). Jesus had just asked the Apostles who men thought He was. It was a good question, and we see Jesus listening for their answer. It was Simon who said, "You are the Christ, the Son of the living God" (Matt. 16:16). Jesus responded quickly. He told all the Apostles that the Father had revealed this secret to Simon and then for the first time in history, an ordinary, everyday word that meant "rock" became a name—Peter. Jesus promised us that this Church would last till the end of time and all Hell would not prevail against it. The Church was then as it is now, an assembly of faithful followers of Jesus as Lord. As Jesus appointed Peter head, the other Apostles looked to him from that moment as the one who had the responsibility of this assembly of people, the Church. It was Peter whom Jesus asked to feed His sheep and lambs Peter who was given the keys of the kingdom to bind and loose, Peter who boldly preached to the crowds on Pentecost, Peter who punished Ananias and Sapphira for their deceit, Peter who made the final decision as to circumcision, Peter whom Paul sought out to assure himself that what he taught was correct.

There was a special deference for Peter among the Apostles, and we see this at the Resurrection. John was much younger than Peter. He arrived at the tomb before him, but waited—waited until Peter arrived and entered first (John 20:3–6). This deference is even more pronounced when we consider Peter had denied Jesus, had fallen deeply on a personal level. His human weaknesses had, for a fearful moment, overtaken him, and he was less than a leader should be. John, however, saw something in Peter that human weakness could not diminish, and that was authority. That authority was given by the Father, and only the Father could take it away. Peter's personal faults were something between him and God, but at that moment John saw the Vicar of Christ, and only that Vicar would go into the tomb to assure himself and all ages after him that the Christ had truly risen.

As it was then, so it is now: it is the prerogative of his successor to pronounce other mysteries of God to the people in order to assure that assembly of the truths God reveals.

After the Resurrection Jesus appeared to Mary Magdalene, the holy women, and the disciples going to Emmaus, but the credibility gap disappeared only when the disciples heard the Eleven assembled together declare, "Yes, it is true. The Lord has risen and has appeared to Peter" (Luke 24:34). The greatest mystery of Faith in the Christian religion was declared by the Eleven with Peter as their leader. Peter, who had special light

from the Father to declare the Messiahship of Jesus, declared
the Resurrection of Jesus because he had seen Him. There was
no question about Peter's special gifts from God. He was set
aside to declare the mysteries of God and the will of God to the
assembly. This was a gift from the Father to Peter and was not
dependent upon Peter's holiness, personality, temperament,
or character. He had his weakness, but when He spoke as one
with special authority — it was the Lord speaking.

When Ananias and Sapphira lied to Peter about their sale
of property, Peter said to them, "How can Satan have so possessed you that you should lie to the Holy Spirit?… It is not to
men that you have lied but to God" (Acts 5:3, 4). A strange
statement from a man who just recently committed a greater
sin by denying he knew Jesus. Was the one who was forgiven
much unable to forgive or understand a moment of weakness?
Or was it that Peter was not speaking as a man, but as Peter
the Rock — the Leader? In that capacity he was the Vicar of
Christ. In this light then Peter could rightly say that Ananias
lied to the Spirit. Yes, we must ask ourselves the question, "Do
those who hate the Church know they are only hating themselves, for the Church is the Assembly of people and they are
part of the human race — the soul of the Church? In hating

the Vicar of Christ do they not mock the spirit of Christ as He guides His people?"

"He has put all things under his feet, and made him, as the ruler of everything, the head of the Church; which is his body, the fullness of him who fills the whole creation" (Eph. 1:22–23). Paul told the Ephesians that by redeeming us Jesus broke down the barrier that kept the Jews and Gentiles apart. Through the Cross he reconciled all mankind to the Father and drew them together into a single Body.

Paul explained at length that we are "no longer aliens among a chosen people" but brothers who share the same Father. "Through Him, both of us [Jews and gentiles] have in the one Spirit our way to the Father" (see Eph. 2:18, 19). This single Body may be rent asunder by dissension, false prophets, heresies, or schism, but that Body the Church continues to seek out, care for, provide for, and protect its members. This mystery of the Church was deep indeed for the first Christians. The chosen people were accustomed to being set apart as the minority who knew the true God. Now, Paul is telling them that Jesus came and died for all men, and through His Bride, the Church, all mankind had the opportunity to know God and His mysteries. Salvation for all men was shocking news for the chosen people. "This mystery," Paul continued to explain, "has now been revealed through the Spirit to His holy apostles and prophets" (Eph. 3:4–5).

It is here that Paul gives us the twofold mission of the Church and Her ordained priests. "I, who am less than the least of all the saints, have been entrusted with this special grace, not only of proclaiming to the pagans the infinite treasure of Christ but also of explaining how the mystery is to be dispensed" (Eph. 3:8). People must not only hear the message, but also hear an explanation of that message. They need to know how to apply the message to daily life. These applications and interpretations are to bear the stamp of truth, for Jesus is truth. God is bound in justice to give His people the truth in regard to every facet of Christian living.

"I wanted you to know," Paul said, "how people ought to behave in God's family, that is, in the Church of the living God, which holds the truth and keeps it safe" (1 Tim. 3:15). Yes, holy Mother Church proclaims, declares, explains, and keeps the truth safe from the reach of the Enemy.

To despise such a Mother is to hate oneself, water down the nourishment that feeds the soul, and hold one's neighbor in contempt. We insult the Christ whose Spirit guides the Church. This Body, the Church, began with the flowing of His Precious Blood and the outpouring of His Spirit. It is no small offense to criticize, ridicule, or downgrade something that is so dear to the Heart of God and for whom He gave so much.

When family life decays, so does love for the Church. The family and the Church are interwoven as one large family composed of many individual families. The union of heart, the love and concern, the mutual upbuilding of members is the same in both.

Family life is based on the same spiritual foundation as the Church. Paul explained this as a mystery and told the first Christians that a man must love his wife in the same way Christ loves His Bride, the Church. "He made her clean by washing her in water [Baptism] with the form of words, so that when he took her to himself she would be glorious, with no speck or wrinkle or anything like that, but holy and faultless" (Eph. 5:25–27). This is how a husband is to love his wife, for if he hates her, he hates himself. "A man never hates his own body, but he feeds it and looks after it; and that is the way Christ treats the Church, because it is his body and we are its living parts" (Eph. 5:28–30).

So it is with the Church as She feeds us with the Sacraments and builds us up with sound doctrine and truth, we in turn become living images of Her Spouse, Jesus. We spring forth from Bride and Bridegroom, bearing the likeness of the Father and the seal of the Spirit on our souls. When we are faithful and true sons and daughters of this holy Mother, our family life will begin to reflect the peace, joy, harmony, and love this Mother places in our souls.

When we hate Her we only hate ourselves, for we are part of Her Body and Jesus is our Head. To alienate ourselves from Him and His Bride is to cut ourselves off from the Vine. How can we possibly expect the return of family harmony when we despise the source of harmony?

We must be zealous to spread Her message, fervent so we may radiate that message, loving so others may see that message in our lives, loyal so that message is obeyed no matter how difficult. When this spirit of love and zeal possesses our hearts, we will all have the courage to be yeast in the dough of our families and mankind.

Change begins with individuals, radiates to others, and in turn gives them the courage to change. Harmony, loyalty, love, and peace in the Church and in the family must grow together. In proportion as one or the other succeeds or fails, in that proportion will each bear fruit or decay.

The Spirit who guides the Church will bear fruit in Church and families together as they are the Body of Christ on earth.

"Now the Church is his body, he is its head.... I am suffering now, in my own body to do what I can to make up all that has still to be undergone by Christ for the sake of his body, the Church" (Col. 1:18, 24). "The saints [the faithful] together make a unity in the work of service, building up the body of Christ" (Eph. 4:12). Yes, we all work together, building, giving hope, courage, and strength to Church and family—the Body of Christ.

CONFIRMATION AND THE HOLY SPIRIT

I Am His Temple

The Seven Gifts of the Holy Spirit are given to me to enhance His Temple — my soul.

The foundation of this Temple is Faith, Hope, and Love, and the Seven Gifts are the tools and material used by the Spirit to construct a fit dwelling place for Jesus to abide in.

I must cooperate with the Spirit in order to manifest to my neighbor a house in which Jesus takes up His abode on earth.

"As every structure is aligned on Him, all grow into one holy Temple in the Lord, and you, too, in Him, are being built into a house where God lives, in the Spirit" (Eph. 2:21–22).

Some of the Gifts — Fear of the Lord, Piety, Fortitude, and Counsel — are used as Tools and Material to reshape the original design. Others, such as Knowledge, Understanding, and Wisdom, constitute the furnishings, and these make the Temple beautiful to behold.

I must remember that tools, materials, and furnishings are Gifts from the Spirit, but they are in my hands, and the house I reshape for Jesus to dwell in will depend upon how I use the supplies.

I can build a shack, a house, a mansion, or a castle, and He will dwell in whatever I build, but since this is a living house, it will edify my neighbor in proportion as the house resembles its Occupant — Jesus.

St. Paul said, "On this foundation [Christ] you can build in gold, silver, and jewels, or in wood, grass, and straw. But whatever the material, the work of each builder is going to be clearly revealed when the day comes" (1 Cor. 3:12–13).

This Temple must be built on the rock of humility, not the sand of pride.

The foundation must be a mixture of Faith, Hope, and Love — in God and not in the world.

The tools I use to change the original dwelling, made of straw and grass, into a castle of jewels must be used under His guidance and not my own.

The furnishings must be carved with the greatest care by the hand of God, and not my hand.

All in all, the Temple of the Lord that His Spirit has made me must be beautiful, changed, and transformed, that it may glorify the Father for all Eternity.

SCRIPTURE

Did you not realize that you were God's Temple and that the Spirit of God was living among you? If anyone should destroy the Temple of God, God will destroy him, because the Temple of God is Sacred, and you are that Temple. (1 Cor. 3:16–17)

Your body, you know, is the Temple of the Holy Spirit, who is in you since you received Him from God. (1 Cor. 6:19)

The Tools and Materials

At Baptism I was made a child of God and the Temple of His Spirit. This is the Good News. Jesus merited this undreamed-of privilege for me.

Is this Presence of God in my soul static, or is it alive? It must be alive and active if its power to transform is going to accomplish its task.

However, a power that I am not aware of is no power at all, so I must see what the Divine Presence of the Trinity means in my everyday life.

Love must manifest itself, and the God who dwells in my soul is Love. He gives me powerful helps that we call "Gifts"—to aid me in my relationship with Him and with my neighbor.

These Gifts are also tools, given to me at Baptism to cooperate with the action of the Spirit in my soul.

They are tremendous aids that take up when my weak virtue ends. They are like the arm of God upholding me in time of need.

I must understand what these Gifts are and what they do for me. They are the higher Gifts that make me bear fruit—fruit that is lasting.

The knowledge of these Gifts and the effort to use them in my daily life will be a powerful means of attaining holiness of life.

The Holy Spirit dwells in me that I may bear fruit and glorify the Father. He is the other Advocate whom Jesus spoke of so many times.

He is sent by Jesus to fill me with love, so that I may love my neighbor and keep the "New Commandment" to love as Jesus loves.

It is important for me to understand that I cannot give love unless I possess love. The love I have must go beyond the natural level to the supernatural level.

I cannot accomplish this unless God and I have a continuous and personal relationship — a relationship of Love, Understanding, and dialogue.

I must know the role of the Holy Spirit in my life in order to correspond with His grace and inspirations.

Jesus said that with Him in me I would bear fruit that would last; without Him I could do nothing.

In order to bear the fruit of good works I must do all I can to preserve my union with Jesus.

I am a branch and cannot bear fruit if I am separated from the vine. My dying to self and living in Jesus will give me the unselfish love so necessary to bear fruit in season and out of season. I will look in the Gospels and see what Jesus said of the other Advocate and find out what His role is in my life with God. I must be sure that the storehouse of my good works is unending, unfailing, and unselfish.

35

Jesus told me during the Last Supper discourse that it was necessary for Him to return to the Father, because then He would send another Advocate — the Holy Spirit.

He said the Spirit would teach me all things, bring to mind the revelations and examples of His life, and, wonder of wonders, the Spirit would make His home in me.

It is the work of the Holy Spirit to make me holy. He it is who diffuses grace into my soul and slowly transforms me into Jesus.

He covers the wounds made by the Father's pruning shears with the balm of love, peace, and joy.

He upholds me in times of temptation with Fear of the Lord, giving me the sense of fear springing from love, a spirit of reverence that prevents me from yielding to temptation.

He gives me patience by the Gift of Piety when my neighbor demands more time and love than I possess.

He strengthens me with Fortitude when I feel too weak to accomplish the tasks He has given me.

He helps me discern, with the Gift of Counsel, when I must decide what is His Will for me.

He detaches me from the things of this world with the Gift of Knowledge.

He increases my Faith by giving me light through the Gift of Understanding.

He thrills my soul with a deep awareness of the Presence of the Lord through the Gift of Wisdom.

These marvelous Gifts are qualities and impulses that set the sail of my boat toward the gentle breeze of the Spirit, Who guides my vessel through the sea of life with ease.

The rudder of my boat is in my hand, and I can go against the wind and take the risk of running aground, or I can follow the mysterious breeze, never sure where it leads, but full of confidence that it is aimed at the shore where the Father and Son await my landing.

During my journey home, these interior Gifts of the Spirit bear much fruit for my neighbor to see and benefit by. When my neighbor sees me kind and patient, he realizes it is some invisible quality that is pleasing to behold and desirable to possess. In this way I glorify the Father and bear witness that Jesus is Lord.

I must look at these Gifts and Fruits and see how I can follow His inspirations with more profit, and glorify the Father by bearing more and more fruit, for the Gifts are tools that I possess and the Spirit uses, to sculpt the cold marble of my soul into the warm, loving image of Jesus.

SCRIPTURE

And there shall come forth a rod out of the root of
Jesse, and a flower shall rise up out of this root. And
the Spirit of the Lord shall rest upon him: the Spirit of
Wisdom and of Understanding, the Spirit of Counsel
and of Fortitude, the Spirit of Knowledge and of Godli-
ness (Piety). And he shall be filled with the Spirit of
the Fear of the Lord. (Isa. 11:1–3)

Spirit of Fear of the Lord

- Horror of Sin
- Filial relationship with God as Father
- Hope — preserves me from presumption or despair

This Gift confuses me at times because to fear and to love seem
so contrary. I am told by St. John that God is Love, and since
the Spirit proceeds from God, He also is Love.

This fear that is instilled in me by Love must be united to
Love in the same way as Mercy is united to Justice.

Looking at it in this light, it seems that I must have a loving
fear of ever offending such a good and kind Father.

By giving me an awareness of God's Goodness in my regard, the Holy Spirit instills within my soul a horror of sin, because only sin can separate me from my Father.

As I begin to see His action and Providence in my daily life I realize how fortunate I am to be called to live in such intimate union with God.

The very thought of doing anything to terminate that union, or even lessen it in the smallest degree, becomes an intolerable suffering. This kind of suffering is not based on scrupulosity, because I realize God's Mercy is infinite and He understands my desires and sees my efforts. But it is built on the foundation of Love — a Love that never wants to be separated from the Beloved.

In order to keep my soul in a perfect balance between fear and love, the Holy Spirit increases in my soul the Virtue of Hope.

Hope is that marvelous virtue that keeps me from despair and presumption.

Without Hope, I would never see the end of the road or the Joy when I finally arrive.

There are times when after a fall my fear of having offended God becomes out of balance — I think my sin is too great for

Him to forgive. Hope comes to the rescue and assures me that in His Love and Mercy He forgives and forgets. He lovingly awaits my return, and all of Heaven rejoices.

There are other times that my fear of offending God almost disappears and I feel a certain lethargy in staying away from occasions of sin, thinking and rationalizing that since God is loving and merciful He really doesn't care about sin at all.

Now it is that Hope brings back my Gift of Fear of the Lord. Somewhere out of the gray clouds of presumption comes the light of God's Justice, and I realize that no matter what I think, God's holiness detects the shadow of sin and I run the risk of losing everlasting happiness for the sake of self-indulgence.

How good God is to give me His Holy Spirit to supply what I need to strive for holiness. I must not stray to the right or left but keep to the middle of the road — straight as an arrow — to arrive at a humble detachment from myself. This will keep me from despair and from presumption.

PRAYER

Holy Spirit, increase this Gift of Loving Fear and Reverence for the Father. Grant that I may never presume on His Mercy, or despair because of His Justice. Let my love for such a good Father fill my soul with childlike Hope because His Mercy supplies for what His Justice demands.

How I can grow in this Gift of Fear of the Lord . . .

. . . with the Father:

When any occasion arises to act unlike my Father, I will immediately call to mind God's Infinite Mercy so that if I fall I will never despair. I will recall at the same time His Infinite Justice so that I will never be spiritually lazy, should I be tempted to presumption. He deserves my very best because He is so good, and I must remember He has called me to great things—I must not be satisfied with crumbs.

. . . in the Son:

Though He loved the sinner, Jesus had a horror of sin, and it cost Him a very humiliating and painful death. He repeatedly encouraged men to repent, not for His sake, but for theirs. He loved me so much, He was willing to show me how to overcome my weakness by realizing more each day the Father's Infinite Love. He kept His eyes on the Father and had the strength to overcome the temptation of the enemy in the desert, the hatred of His people, and the ingratitude of His friends. I will follow in His footsteps and stay away from any occasion of sin.

. . . through the Spirit:

I must put all my trust in the power of the Holy Spirit to give me strength. His inspirations are quiet and gentle, so I must keep my soul in peace in order to hear His Voice. He is ready to assist me immediately with His powerful grace if only I cry out for help when I feel my weakness.

Holy Spirit, give me an increase of the Gift of the Fear of the Lord that I may never willfully offend God.

SCRIPTURE

The fear of the Lord is glory and pride, and happiness and a crown of joyfulness.

The fear of the Lord will gladden the heart giving happiness and joy and long life.

With him who fears the Lord it will be well at the last and he will be blessed on the day of his death.

To fear the Lord is the beginning of Wisdom; she was created with the faithful in her mother's womb.

She has made a nest among men, an age-old foundation, and to her offspring she will cling faithfully.

To fear the Lord is the perfection of Wisdom; she intoxicates them with her fruits;

She fills their whole house with their hearts' desire, and their storerooms with her produce.

The fear of the Lord is the crown of Wisdom; it makes peace and health to flourish.

The Lord has looked on her and assessed her. He has showered down learning and discernment, and exalted the renown of those who hold her close.

To fear the Lord is the root of Wisdom, and her branches are long life. (Sir. 1:11–25)

Spirit of Piety

- God is my Father
- All men are brothers
- Patience

When I begin to have a loving fear of offending God, the Holy Spirit instills in my soul a deep awareness that God is my Father.

This awareness is something almost tangible because it permits me to cry out, "Abba, Father" with conviction and love (see Rom. 8:15).

This Gift gives me the push I need to begin an intimate life of union with God—a life of a son speaking to and loving a Father.

Whereas the Gift of Fear of the Lord has given me a child-like fear of God, this Gift of Piety gives me a childlike affection for God. I begin to accomplish God's Will out of a deep affection—an awareness of an invisible bond drawing us close together in a tie nothing can break.

God's honor and glory become the goal of my life, and I begin to think more of Him and less of myself.

I desire to bear fruit as Jesus said I would when I give myself entirely to the Father. This Gift, like the others, was so beautiful in Jesus; I must desire to imitate Him in His great zeal for the Father's honor and glory.

Jesus told me that God is my Father and I can do nothing without Him. This is the truth, but He sent me His Spirit to assure me that I can do all things with Him and this is the Way.

Jesus tells me how to glorify the Father, and the Spirit gives me the means to glorify the Father through the Gift of Piety.

Jesus loved the Father above all things, and loved me enough to give His life for me.

This Gift, then, has a twofold effect on my soul: it gives me a spirit of sonship with God and a spirit of brotherhood with my neighbor.

Because the Trinity lives within me, I am able to love my neighbor with the same love and in the same way as the Father loves Jesus.

Piety gives me the power to see beyond the human defects of my neighbor to the image of the Father.

It is an invisible strength that is not overpowered by the faults and sins of others. It manages in some mysterious way to see God's Essence in the worst and most depraved, and God's Presence in the good and holy.

This Gift seems to bring with it a certain amount of honesty — it doesn't cover over my neighbor's sins, or defects, or peculiarities; it sees them all clearly. These very weaknesses elicit greater love and compassion, for Piety sees in all this misery the opportunity to imitate the Father and Jesus, whose love is given to all.

In His Humanity, Jesus possessed and used this Gift to the fullest. He never seemed surprised at the miserable depths to which human nature could descend, and neither was His Love lessened by the sight.

The Gift of Piety made Him give His Life for His friends who were sinners — and everyone was His friend.

He was no respecter of persons. His Love reached out to rich and poor, sick and healthy, young and old, sinner and saint.

It is because Jesus possessed this Gift of Piety in the highest degree that the Holy Spirit gives it to me, for it is His work to transform me into Jesus. I must possess all the Gifts of the Spirit because Jesus merited this opportunity for me — the opportunity to possess in a finite way what He possesses in an infinite way.

Piety will help me to think more of my neighbor's good than my own, and will give me the power to continue to seek His good in the face of insult and ingratitude.

I will love, not because I will be loved in return, but because, like Jesus, I will be filled with love, and love reaches out to give.

Through the Gift of Piety, the Holy Spirit gives me the desire to imitate Jesus and His Love for His neighbor.

I cannot say I love the Father whom I do not see if I do not love my neighbor whom I see (see 1 John 4:20), and Piety aids me in this quest of seeing the Invisible All-Holy God in visible, unholy human beings.

PRAYER

Holy Spirit, let me grow in this beautiful Gift of Piety so I may seek the Father's honor and glory by radiating the self-less love of Jesus to my neighbor.

How I can grow in this Gift of Piety . . .

   . . . with the Father:

I will often think of the Father's immanence and try to realize that God is in everything and everyone, either through His Essence inasmuch as He keeps all creatures in existence, or through Grace as He dwells in the souls of the just.

I must go further and not only see vestiges of Him in creation and His Image in my neighbor, but must do all I can to bear fruit in order to manifest the perfection of God in my daily life, especially His Goodness.

I will grow in the Gift of Piety by bringing to mind in trying situations that God is in my neighbor and I must treat him on that level, and not on the level of his merits.

   . . . in the Son:

Jesus excelled in this Gift because He is God's Son, but I must not forget that He merited this same privilege for me through Grace. I, too, can and must excel in the Gift of Piety by loving my neighbor whether or not he loves me in return.

Jesus was so patient with the faults of His Apostles, not because they did not irritate Him, but because He understood their weakness and had compassion with their frailties.

This understanding love made Him patient. He was willing to wait while those He loved grew in their acceptance of Him and in the strength they needed to stand by their convictions.

He had only one thing in mind—the Father's honor and glory and His desire to have His loved ones with Him in the Kingdom.

His love for the Father and all the Father's children made Him pray without ceasing, labor without rest, suffer without complaint, do good without gratitude, give without acceptance, and die without friends. I will follow in His footsteps.

. . . *through the Holy Spirit:*

I must ask the Holy Spirit for more of this Gift every day. It is difficult to love everyone, and yet my degree of love of God is based on my love for my neighbor.

I need a generous portion of patience to accept the imperfections of my neighbor without lessening my love for him.

My inability to love my neighbor at times is often caused by my lack of patience. I think he should grow immediately, but I give myself time and excuses to rise and fall in my journey to holiness.

I will use the tool of Piety and see beyond my neighbor's imperfections — not because it is easy, but because I have the Holy Spirit within me and His Power can accomplish all things in me.

Holy Spirit, give me the Gift of Piety that I may love without counting the cost.

SCRIPTURE

Bear with one another charitably, in complete selflessness, gentleness, and patience. Do all you can to preserve the unity of the Spirit by the peace that binds you together. There is one Body, one Spirit, just as you were all called into one and the same hope when you were called. There is one Lord, one Faith, one Baptism, and one God who is Father of all, over all, through all, and within all.

Each one of us, however, has been given his own share of grace, given as Christ allotted it. It was said that He would: "When He ascended to the height, He captured prisoners, He gave gifts to men." (Eph. 4:2–8)

Spirit of Fortitude

- ☞ Courage in Suffering
- ☞ Perseverance in doing good
- ☞ Prudence

Each Gift seems to blend and support the other Gifts, and so it is with the Gift of Fortitude.

This is a very important quality to possess because it makes me persevere in my pursuit of holiness.

I tend to become discouraged when, after exerting so much effort to love my neighbor and stay away from sin, I fall repeatedly.

The real problem at times is not so much that I doubt God's forgiveness but whether or not I have the strength to continue fighting what seems to be a losing battle.

Here it is that the Holy Spirit gives me Fortitude — the strength to continue forging ahead in the face of opposition, failure, falls, and weakness.

Perhaps it's a kind of holy stubbornness where great desires overcome my lack of ability and the awareness that, no matter how hard I try, I cannot do it alone.

To keep on fighting for Christian principles when everyone around me tells me to follow the crowd, demands a power from God Himself, and that Power is Fortitude.

It is in the realm of the spiritual life where the Gift of Fortitude aids me the most. There are times when I can practice virtue rather easily, but there are other times when the occasion of sin is greater than my own strength allows, and it is at these times — when heroism is called for — that the Holy Spirit gives me the extra strength I need.

It is the very strength of God, poured into my soul by the Holy Spirit, that comes to my aid and literally supports my weakness.

"My Power is at its best in weakness," said Jesus to Paul — and this is Fortitude (2 Cor. 12:9).

Fortitude gives me the power to persevere in doing good, but it also gives me supernatural endurance.

It is one thing to accept the cross; but when there is no end in view and the cross gets heavier, then the Spirit of Fortitude gives me the power to endure the things I can neither change nor eliminate.

I can accept a headache with comfortable ease knowing it will be better tomorrow, but if it were a painful cancer, I would have to ask for the Spirit of Fortitude.

I can accept a difficult personality for an hour or so, but if it's for a lifetime, I need the Gift of Fortitude.

I can accept privation for a month or so, but if it goes on for years, I need the Gift of Fortitude.

I can accept misunderstanding for a little while, but when it turns into hatred and I am helpless to correct it, I need the Gift of Fortitude.

I can accept injustice, knowing we don't all think alike, but when it deprives me of freedom, I need the Gift of Fortitude.

I can accept prejudice once in a while, realizing some don't understand, but when it takes away my dignity, I need the Gift of Fortitude.

This brings me to another aspect of Fortitude — the ability to wait.

It takes an inner power to wait and maintain any semblance of serenity.

When I must wait for ...

- the conversion of a friend
- the return of health, mine or others
- the recognition of a job well done
- the arrival of a loved one
- the settlement of a dispute
- the forgiveness of a friend
- reconciliation with an enemy

- the cessation of a pain
- the control of my own weaknesses
- the time when all men will be brothers
- the journey's end

… then I need the Gift of Fortitude.

The Holy Spirit goes further and gives me the courage to undertake great things for God. There is a holy daring that accompanies Fortitude—a daring that pushes aside difficulties and even the impossible, and seeks only the good of the Kingdom.

Lest I develop pride because of the difficult things I do or a martyr complex over the painful things I endure, the Holy Spirit unites joy to Fortitude.

Joy makes it easier—so easy sometimes that I can, as the Master said in the Eight Beatitudes, exult with exceeding Joy over my misery.

PRAYER

Holy Spirit, sweet Guest of my soul, I need the Gift of Fortitude to persevere, to endure, to wait, to undertake great things, and to be filled with Joy. Give me the strength to be selfless and totally Thine.

How I can grow in this Gift of Fortitude . . .

. . . with the Father:

When difficulties crowd in upon me and I am so helpless, I will go to a quiet place and think about the Father's Omnipotence. He is so powerful that nothing is impossible to Him. If the heavy cross I bear is not lifted by His loving hands, then I know He loves me enough to treat me as a son, and He wants me to draw good out of this cross. He would not permit it otherwise. The contemplation of His great Power will draw down upon my poor soul great courage and strength. I will be like an empty vessel being filled with the very strength of God.

. . . in the Son:

Jesus gave me many examples of Fortitude.

He continued to do good, despite the opposition of the leaders of His day.

He cured and healed in the face of ingratitude and criticism.

He labored for the good of the Kingdom and bore great fruit to glorify the Father.

He endured physical and mental torments to merit the grace of His Spirit, giving me the Gift of Fortitude.

He accomplished the impossible by building His Church on the abilities of twelve weak men — as one betrayed Him,

His chosen leader denied Him, and all the others ran when He was in need.

In the face of utter failure, He rose from the grave, and He gave His own Spirit, knowing that even then many would not accept Him. He was unheralded but undaunted. I will follow in His footsteps.

. . . through the Holy Spirit:

The Gift of Fortitude seems to touch so many facets of my life. I must pray daily for an increase of this Gift, and I will use it during those difficult moments when my own strength seems to be ebbing away.

I need only call upon the Holy Spirit Himself to accomplish and endure those things that are beyond my strength.

He wants to give me much more than I can ask for, so I must not hesitate to be daring and ask for the very heights of holiness.

Holy Spirit, give me the Gift of Fortitude that I may do great things for the Kingdom.

SCRIPTURE

Think of what Christ suffered in this life, and then arm yourselves with the same resolution that He had:

anyone who in this life has bodily suffering has broken with sin, because for the rest of his life on earth he is not ruled by human passions but only by the Will of God. (1 Pet. 4:1–2)

If you can have some share in the sufferings of Christ, be glad, because you will enjoy a much greater gladness when His glory is revealed. It is a blessing for you when they insult you for bearing the Name of Christ, because it means that you have the Spirit of Glory, the Spirit of God, resting on you. (1 Pet. 4:13–14)

Spirit of Counsel

- ☞ Discernment
- ☞ Self-knowledge and Mercy
- ☞ Brings to mind Christ's teaching

There are times in my life when I must make decisions, discern what is from the Holy Spirit, my own spirit, or the evil spirit; be prudent in my dealings and works, be strong enough to see myself as I really am, and recall the life of Jesus — in order to draw courage for my daily life.

To accomplish all this, the Holy Spirit gives me the Gift of Counsel. It is a very powerful Gift because it lets me see myself and others in their true light.

I will look at the different aspects of this Gift to see how I can use it for greater progress in holiness.

The Master said many times that there would be false prophets, false Christs, and wolves in sheep's clothing. My soul must be open to the Spirit so He can give me that kind of intuition and light to penetrate the incident or person and see truth.

There are false doctrines, capable of destroying my soul, and I need the light of discernment to penetrate the beautiful exterior and see the darkness of error.

There are different works that seem good, and I must discern whether my motive for such works is my own pride or the glory of God.

There are people who keep encouraging me to take the easy road, and their arguments seem reasonable, but I must discern that the road to holiness is difficult to travel and take courage from Jesus, who walked it before me.

I wonder sometimes if Jesus did not have discernment in mind when He said I must be as cunning as serpents, yet as harmless as doves (Matt. 10:16).

The Tempter will cross my path many times, and I must discern his tactics, his presence, and his temptations to be hateful, unforgiving, jealous, greedy, ambitious for worldly things, and proud. I must see these things as they really are—temptations. I cannot rationalize them and blame other people. I must discern that no matter what occasion or person causes these feelings, it is the tempter who makes them linger and eat at my soul.

I must stay very close to my Friend, the Spirit, in order to have both the light and the strength to discern good from evil, right from wrong, the human spirit from the Holy Spirit, and an opportunity to practice virtue from an occasion to sin.

I need to be detached from my own opinions in order to be open to the quiet inspirations of the Holy Spirit. Only then will I be able to discern what He is saying and what He desires.

Almost every day there are some decisions to make, and there are times when I must make a choice that may prove painful.

How I need the Spirit of Counsel to give me the light to see where God's Will lies!

The Gift of Counsel clears the fog of uncertainty and gives me a clear picture of the right course to take and the determination to follow that course to a successful conclusion.

Only the surety that comes from the Gift of Counsel can give me that holy audacity to accomplish great things for God.

Because the Gift of Counsel can give me a great impetus to go all out for God, the Spirit joins Prudence with Counsel. Prudence guides me and permits me to discern the difference between an action that may be foolhardy and one that is inspired.

Perhaps the most important effect of the Gift of Counsel is self-knowledge. It gives me the light I need to see myself as I really am.

It takes a special quality to see my faults and not rationalize them or pretend they are not there. I can go through life under an illusion and adhere to my own opinions to the extent that everyone is wrong except myself.

The basest actions can be rationalized until they no longer seem wrong. How much I need the Gift of Counsel to see that my anger or impatience are mine and cannot be excused on the pretext that my neighbor or circumstances cause my failures! I cannot blame people or things even though they supplied the opportunity. I must look beyond the incident and discern the form of Jesus and the Will of the Father, and see only the pruning shears of virtue reshaping my soul into the image of Christ.

I will look deep and see that:

- my pride makes me rebel against ingratitude and insult
- my impatience refuses to wait
- my anger seeks excuses to vent its fury
- my lack of faith makes me doubt His Love
- my ambition makes me pretentious
- my lethargy makes me give up
- my envy rejoices at another's misfortune
- my unkindness makes me rude
- my lack of mercy makes me critical
- my lack of love makes me unbearable

So I must practice mental discipline and not permit any kind of disturbance to enter my soul. I must, as the Master suggests, shake the dust from my soul and be sure my peace returns to me when it is not accepted by my neighbor. This sounds easier than it is, but I must have Faith in the Spirit and my own ability to overcome whatever I set my will to accomplish.

Whenever anything happens that hurts me and I notice it begins to occupy my mind, I must have immediate recourse to prayer, be it ever so short. I must raise my thoughts to God's Mercy, Love, and Patience, or recall the life of Jesus in order to calm my imagination and emotions.

It is here that the Holy Spirit, through the gift of Counsel, instills within my Understanding and Will, more control of the situation and of my own thoughts.

If I permit my memory to constantly recall the incident and incite my imagination to exaggerate everything out of proportion, my understanding becomes unreasonable and my will weak — the incident is in control of me and not I in control of it.

The inspirations of the Spirit are literally squelched by the outpouring of impatience, hatred, anger, and pride. How can I possibly benefit by the quiet whisperings of the Spirit under such uncontrolled emotions?

I must quiet my imagination and memory by prayer and looking at Jesus. The Holy Spirit will then give me the light to see my own weakness and the tactics of the tempter in different situations so I can rise above them, offer them to the Father in union with Jesus, and overcome them through the power of the Spirit.

It is of prime importance that I see God in everything and hear His Voice as He calls me to repentance, humility, love, patience, and kindness.

Every trying situation is an appeal from God to imitate His Son.

Every person in need presents an invitation to call upon the power of His Spirit.

Every weakness is an opportunity to depend upon His strength.

Every pain is a call to imitate Jesus and to endure with patience.

Every lonely hour invites me to remember the ever-present Guest of my soul and be comforted.

Every persecution is an occasion to bless, forgive, and rejoice that I have been found worthy to imitate Jesus.

Every misunderstanding enables me to be compassionate and merciful.

My whole life, from moment to moment, is a call from God to answer, "Here I am to do Thy Will."

I need the Gift of Counsel to live in the light of discernment so I may face the truth unafraid, by always keeping my hand in His.

RECALLING THE LIFE OF JESUS

Perhaps this is the most important effect of the Gift of Counsel in my life. It is the work of the Spirit to recall to my mind the life, revelations, and sayings of Jesus, at those times when I need them.

Jesus went so far as to say that I was not even to prepare my defense or wonder what to say when the occasion to speak in His Name arose. He told me the Spirit would give me eloquence and tell me what to say.

It is the same with my faults and weaknesses. He not only reveals them to me, but He gives me the remedy for all my spiritual ills — the example of Jesus.

No matter how difficult things may be, there is a parallel in the life of Jesus. I can see how He acted and what He said and can base my actions on that knowledge rather than on my emotions.

I am not to pretend to be Jesus. I must be myself in every circumstance, but I can regulate my life and actions by the principles He laid down for me.

The Gospels are full of examples of virtue in every possible situation, and through the Gift of Counsel the Spirit will recall those incidents with such clarity that I will know how to act and what to say.

There may be times when it will be necessary to search for an answer to a problem, but I need never fear — His Counsel will guide me.

I must read the Gospels daily in order to absorb the Word into my soul. His Gospels are more than an example of what He accomplished; they give me the power to imitate that example and duplicate it in my own life.

The reading of His Life and the inspirations of His Spirit help to change my life when I observe:

- His patience under trying circumstances
- His love in the face of ingratitude
- His indifference to the slander of His enemies
- His compassion for sinners
- His forbearance with the faults of His friends
- His humility in the face of arrogance
- His kindness to those in need
- His forgiveness to those who offended Him
- His just anger when His Father's House was made a den of thieves
- His desire to sacrifice His Life for sinners

PRAYER

Holy Spirit, my Friend and Counselor, fill me more each day with this necessary Gift of Counsel. Enlighten my mind that I may think thoughts of peace, discern Thy Will and

Action, mix zeal with prudence, know myself, and absorb within my soul the love and virtues of Jesus.

How I can grow in this Gift of Counsel . . .

. . . with the Father:

I will often think of the Father's Wisdom and Omniscience. He knows all things and nothing happens to me that has not passed through His Hands. He measured it, looked at every detail, and gave it to me.

Even the evil in my life is permitted only because within it there is some good.

I will ask my Father for light when I must make a decision and realize that He will answer my prayer. If I should make the wrong decision, He will stand by me and give me the graces I need to make all things right.

He has a definite plan for me, and I must ask Him for the light to see His Will clearly.

. . . in the Son:

Jesus always knew exactly what the Father willed for Him at every moment. There were times He was severe and times He was merciful. He condemned the Pharisees, and forgave the woman taken in adultery. He discerned that the sins of one stemmed from pride, and the other from weakness. The one He corrected with severity in the hope of bringing out the pride hidden within. For the other He had Mercy in order to give strength to repent and reform.

It is the beautiful virtue of Mercy in Jesus that gave Him a high degree of discernment.

It was Merciful Discernment that made Him

- condemn the lawyers as whited sepulchers — to rouse them to examine their consciences
- forgive the Magdalen, who had seven devils — because she was filled with repentant love
- plead with the man He cured to be careful lest something worse happen to him
- warn Peter that He would deny Him three times
- foretell the Apostles' future persecutions and give them joy to overcome
- see His Father's Will and accomplish it with tranquility even though He realized His words and actions aggravated many
- stand tall for the sake of Justice though He stood alone

I will follow in His Footsteps.

. . . through the Holy Spirit:

I must try to keep my soul quiet in order to hear the voice of the Spirit as He guides me along the path of holiness.

I must realize that there will be times when I will be in great doubt as to what course to take. This very doubt is the beginning of discernment for it is telling me: when in doubt, stand still—wait—the time has not as yet arrived to clearly see the right road.

I need not fear that doubt is an indication that the Spirit has not answered my prayer. He is merely telling me to wait. Sometimes, no action is the best action, and I must trust the Spirit and know I can make a decision only according to the light I have at the moment—and He will stand by me.

I must petition the Spirit for self-knowledge, and not be surprised if the answer is immediate. He often lets me see my faults, not so that I may become discouraged, but so that I may know in what areas I need pruning, so my soul may take on the virtues of Jesus and reflect His Mercy and Love.

Holy Spirit, give me an increase of the Gift of Counsel that I may walk in the paths of holiness all the days of my life.

SCRIPTURE

The Advocate, the Holy Spirit, whom the Father will send in My Name, will teach you everything and remind you of all I have said to you. (John 14:26)

And when He comes, He will show the world how wrong it was, about sin, and about who was in the right, and about judgment: about sin, proved by their refusal to believe in Me; about who was in the right, proved by My going to the Father and your seeing Me no more; about judgment, proved by the prince of this world being already condemned. (John 16:8–11)

But when they hand you over, do not worry about how to speak or what to say. What you are to say will be given to you when the time comes, because it is not you who will be speaking but the Spirit of your Father will be speaking in you. (Matt. 10:19–20)

Spirit of Knowledge

- Detachment and Hope
- Realization of one thing necessary
- Ability to see God in everything

One day Jesus said that it would profit a man nothing if he gained the whole world and lost his own soul (see Matt. 16:26).

There are times in my life when I seem to experience an intuitive knowledge of the one thing necessary.

This is especially true when I can:

- see the balance between loving myself and hating my life lest I lose it
- love my neighbor and not become attached
- use the things of this world and not be possessed by them
- enjoy life without resting in it
- provide for today without undue concern for tomorrow
- have a zest for life and a desire for Heaven
- see God in all things and yet realize He transcends them all
- admire visible beauty without losing sight of its invisible Source

The Spirit gives me a kind of spiritual awareness of the one thing necessary in this life—the transformation of my soul into Jesus, the honor of the Father, and the good of the Kingdom.

It is difficult to love so unselfishly that I seek only the good of my neighbor, and yet, unless I do, I can never really say I love him for himself.

The Gift of Knowledge is not a blinder that obliterates my neighbor's faults; it gives me the power to see beyond the rough exterior and see the image of God.

It elevates my love and concern beyond the visible and sees God, whose Omnipotence and Mercy uphold the sinner, and whose Love supports the just.

Perhaps it is easier to see God in the sinner because I must make a greater effort to do so. It is one of the paradoxes of life that I run the risk of losing sight of God in those people who are easy to love, because I begin to seek them for my own good.

Pleasure and success can envelop me to the point where I no longer see God but only myself. I can become attached to personal glory and desire to be loved for my own sake and not for God's sake.

My own love becomes selfish and my love for others possessive, and then it is that I need to implore the Spirit for the Gift of Knowledge.

The Gift of Knowledge is that ability to love deeply and enjoy the good things of life without undue concern in the event I lose them.

St. Paul put it beautifully when he said it didn't matter to him whether he was praised or blamed providing he never lost sight of Christ.

The reason I need this special knowledge is that it makes me realize the one thing necessary in every facet of life.

I can become entangled in myself and situations and lose sight of what the Lord is trying to teach me.

If someone offends me, I must see beyond the offender and see only God's pruning love permitting evil for my good. However, I must exert some effort to see God in this situation, and then the Holy Spirit will increase the Gift of Knowledge to make it easier.

I begin to realize that every moment of my life is part of a plan, and I see only one thing—God's Will and God's Love for me.

This Gift prevents me from becoming bitter and resentful and from holding grudges. It does not see imperfect people who cause me distress, but only opportunities to be like Jesus.

Psalm 106 says, "He changes desert into streams, thirsty ground into springs of water." I like to think this refers to the effects of the Gift of Knowledge. It changes the many deserts of loneliness and humiliations into the springs of living water that nourish my soul with Grace and the new life.

Within every cross in my life there is a hidden treasure, wrapped in pain, waiting for me to reach out and take it to myself.

The Gift of Knowledge helps me to find the pearl of great price hidden in the soil of adversity. It sees the true wealth of life — the riches that no moth consumes or rust destroys — the love and friendship of God through Jesus, His Son.

It sees that:

- Though I gain the whole world and do not have the love of Jesus in my heart, that wealth would be nothing.
- Though I gave all my money to the poor, without the love of Jesus in my heart, it would be nothing.
- Though I made great discoveries in the field of science but for selfish motives and not the love of Jesus and my neighbor, it would be nothing.
- Though I conquered the world but never conquered myself, it would be nothing.

- ❧ Though I made others walk the straight and narrow path but never controlled myself, it would be nothing.
- ❧ Though I practiced heroic virtue but only to be seen by men and not for love of Jesus, it would be nothing.
- ❧ Though the world applaud me but at the expense of my own soul, it would be nothing.
- ❧ Though I were an intellectual and possessed great knowledge but never knew God, it would be nothing.

But when I begin:

- ❧ to know the one thing necessary in all things
- ❧ to know how to endure all things with love
- ❧ to know how to forgive and forget with mercy
- ❧ to know how to rise above all things with detachment
- ❧ to know how to see God's Plan in all things

then that is Something—that is the Gift of Knowledge.

I can see from this that the Gift of Knowledge brings with it a high degree of Hope. My hope began to increase with the Gift of Fear of the Lord, but in that Gift it was only a kind of balance that kept me from despair or presumption. But with the Gift of Knowledge my Hope becomes deeper, stable, and more joyous.

The Apostles Peter and John portrayed this kind of hope when they rejoiced that they were found worthy to suffer something in imitation of the Master.

They saw more than persecutors and proud Pharisees; they knew these trials were only opportunities to act like sons of the Father.

Most of my problems in life stem from a lack of understanding of the hidden mystery behind every disagreeable circumstance. I must not take everything personally but rather must see people trying hard, though often failing, to be good.

With this Gift, I can look at the most disagreeable situation and retain the hope that comes from seeing the invisible hand of God in it all.

This attitude keeps me from becoming discouraged and disheartened. Things become unbearable when I look only at the situation, find no reason for it, and then take it on a personal level. So often what I consider the shadow of a giant looming ahead to destroy me turns out to be merely my own shadow created by the light of God behind me—directing, correcting, and reshaping me into His Image.

This Gift can give me a sense of freedom in my life. I spend so much time trying to analyze why things happen, the motives behind them, and my own hurt feelings that it is impossible to retain any kind of peace. But when I begin to see God's pruning shears providing or permitting opportunities for me to forgive or love, then I can accept them with peace.

I must train myself to see these opportunities. The Master has asked me to pray for those who offend me and to bless those who curse me. He has not asked the impossible, though at times it seems so. When I begin to understand and see these occasions for what they really are — opportunities to grow in the image of Jesus — then I will be using the Gift of Knowledge as a key that opens many closed doors in my life.

Life will no longer be an endurance test but a journey with the Divine Traveler, who gives me the light of Knowledge in the darkness to guide me Home.

PRAYER

Holy Spirit, increase in me this Gift of Knowledge, that I may penetrate the mystery of pain and suffering in my life. I do not ask to understand the reason behind everything but only the lesson Your Wisdom wishes to teach me.

How I can grow in this Gift of Knowledge . . .

. . . with the Father:

I will often think of the Father's Goodness and Providence. He supplies not only for my material needs but for my spiritual needs. His Goodness brings good out of evil, and His Providence provides many opportunities for good works.

His Goodness rewards me for what His Providence has provided, and His Omnipotence has given me the strength to accomplish.

All things are present to Him in the Eternal Now — and so His Wisdom enlightens me to see the one thing necessary that I may reap the fruit of every joy and sorrow in my life.

He hovers over me with Infinite Care and will not permit anything to happen to me that is not for my good in some way. I must trust Him no matter how hard it is to trust. His Fatherly Love accepts my efforts to see Him in everything even though my faith wavers in the darkness.

. . . in the Son:

This Gift was so manifest in Jesus. He made friends with rich and poor, sinner and saint, and yet He never let His love for them interfere with the Father's Will in their regard.

He knew that following Him meant persecution and suffering for His Apostles, but He never hid that reality from them. In fact, He foretold what their future sufferings would be because of their belief in Him.

He held on to Truth in the most trying circumstances because He wanted to impress upon me the one thing necessary—the glory of the Father and the good of my neighbor—and this at the expense of myself and all I hold dear.

He never became so involved in a painful situation that He lost sight of His Father's Will. He accepted suspicion and ridicule as part of the Father's plan for Him. His loving acceptance made it holy but not painless.

He elevated suffering and made it capable of adding to my eternal glory rather than to my ruin. He gave me courage by His courage, hope by His victories, and faith by His Resurrection.

I will follow in His Footsteps.

. . . through the Holy Spirit:

There are times in life when fear grips my soul and a feeling of futility casts a shadow over everything. The fear of the future with its uncertainties, the burden of the cross with no end in view—all seem to crush in upon me and drain from my soul the last ray of hope.

It is at a time like this that I must beseech the Spirit to increase my Gift of Knowledge. I need His strength to quiet my memory when it brings to mind old resentments that fill my soul with anger and bitterness.

I need His Power to quiet my imagination as it plunges my soul into the fear of what the future will bring and my inability to cope with the present.

The Gift of Knowledge quiets these two faculties because it brings to my mind how God has taken care of me in the past, and assures me that His Providence will provide for me in the future. The present moment holds no terror in it, for I will use this Gift as a tool to free my soul of useless worry and plunge it into the almighty arms of my Father, who watches over me as a mother her only child.

With this Gift I can look into the past and recall successes and failures, virtues and sins. It gives me the light to be humble and praise God for all the good I accomplish, and it reaps the fruit of my mistakes. It makes me understand that the recollection of my weaknesses can be the occasion to grow in humility, patience, and understanding. It knows how to make things turn to my good.

My imagination often works overtime and projects dark pictures of the future, magnifies my neighbor's faults, and nurtures past offenses by imputing evil motives on innocent actions. This is where my Gift of Knowledge can render me a great service. This Gift gives me the assurance that everything I may have suffered unjustly will be rewarded by my Father. Every suffering I bring upon myself He will accept as part of my penance if I give it to Him with love and patience.

My future and all it holds is in the best of Hands. The Gift of Knowledge gives me a deep realization of the purpose of my life, and how important I am to God and the world. I form a definite part of His Plan, and this realization gives me confidence to forge ahead.

I will daily petition the Holy Spirit to increase this important Gift — the Gift that gives me freedom through detachment; the ability to see God in suffering and pain; a consciousness of the one thing necessary; and a confidence in His Divine Providence that guides and plans every facet of my life.

Holy Spirit, increase my Gift of Knowledge, that I may never lose sight of the one thing necessary.

SCRIPTURE

Set your hearts on His Kingdom first, and on His righteousness, and all these other things will be given you as well. So do not worry about tomorrow; tomorrow will take care of itself. Each day has enough trouble of its own. (Matt. 6:33–34)

Martha, Martha, you worry and fret about so many things, and yet few are needed, indeed only one. (Luke 10:41–42)

For Him I have accepted the loss of everything, and I look on everything as so much rubbish if only I can have Christ and be given a place in Him. I am no longer trying for perfection by my own efforts … but I want only the perfection that comes through faith in Christ and is from God and based on faith. (Phil. 3:8–9)

What gain, then, is it for a man to win the whole world and ruin his life? And, indeed, what can a man offer in exchange for his life? (Mark 8:36–37)

If I have the gift of prophecy, understanding all the mysteries there are, and knowing everything, and if I have faith in all its fullness, to move mountains, but without love, then I am nothing at all. (1 Cor. 13:2)

I have seen everything that is done under the sun, and what vanity it all is, what chasing of wind…. I have great experience of wisdom and learning.... And now I have come to recognize that even this is chasing of the wind.... I then reflected on all that my hands had achieved and on all the effort I had put in its achieving. What vanity it all is and chasing of the wind. (Eccles. 1:14, 16; 2:11)

Spirit of Understanding

- Light to penetrate mysteries
- Greater Faith
- Deeper prayer life

As I look at these different Gifts, I can see that each one adds some quality to my spiritual life that is necessary for my advancement in holiness.

Each Gift is distinct and beautiful in itself, and yet they all enfold and enhance each other, forming a strong ladder leading me to God.

I saw in the Gift of Knowledge a quality of detachment and a realization that there is more to life than meets the eye.

The Gift of Understanding continues on and lets me penetrate the invisible realities behind the things that Knowledge has stripped away.

The Spirit does not leave me hanging in midair after He has shown me the vanity of all things in this world; He rouses my Faith to a higher plane so that I may penetrate the mysteries of God.

This does not mean that I understand them fully, for that is impossible for a finite mind.

It does mean, however, that I seem to reach the essence of a mystery so I almost "feel" its meaning.

Understanding does not add anything to God's revelations, but it gives me the ability to "see within" the mystery.

I may not be capable of explaining to others what I see, but it is all very clear in my own soul — clear enough to unite my soul to God in a most beautiful way.

I must realize that it is the Gift of Understanding in operation when I suddenly get some new light on a passage of Scripture that I read a hundred times before and never understood.

These sudden lights that lift my soul to another plane, or give me courage for a difficult task, are all the Gift of Understanding increasing my Faith that I may "see" God.

There is a kind of intuitive Faith about the Gift of Understanding. It raises me above the ordinary beliefs I possess and enables me to see into the core of a mystery.

It's like seeing a full-color picture of a sunrise in a magazine, and looking at one outside my window. Both are a sunrise, yet the beauty of the former is outside of me, and the beauty of the latter has somehow penetrated within me.

My Faith tells me there is a Trinity of Persons in God, and I believe — but if suddenly I realize this mystery is within me, and somehow understand that I really carry these Divine Persons everywhere I go, then this is the Gift of Understanding in operation.

It remains a mystery in itself but it is more real and very close — it is mine, and it affects my whole life by adding a new dimension to my Faith — the kind of Faith that almost "sees."

Passages of Scripture take on new meaning with the Gift of Understanding. It does not add to the literal or historical sense of Scripture, but it gives me a deep spiritual sense of Scripture.

It gives me the capability of applying Scripture to my everyday life, and opens the way for the Lord to speak to me as a friend speaks to a friend.

Perhaps one of the most important effects of the Gift of Understanding is this increase of Faith.

Faith must be more than an intellectual acceptance of God's revelations. It must touch my daily life and affect the life of my neighbor.

When I begin to realize with an unexplainable surety and awareness that:

- there is a God who loves all men, but loves me in a personal way
- God is my Father, and I must look upon my neighbor as a brother
- God is one and yet Three Persons, and each Person affects my life
- God is everywhere, and yet I have only to look within to find Him
- God's Providence cares for everyone, and yet He knows my every move, and provides for me, as a person, with the care of a Father for his only child
- His Love weighs every cross before it is put on my shoulders

then I will be growing in the Gift of Understanding and in living the inner mystery of His Revealing Love.

When I begin to penetrate the mysteries of God, my prayer life will become deeper, quiet and more contemplative.

My Faith will rest secure in the darkness and be content to love and wait.

Prayer will be more than a conversation, between God as Father and myself as child. It will rise to the heights of Lover and Beloved—a new relationship—a relationship of peace and understanding.

There are many kinds and ways of prayer, and I use them all at different times and stages in my life of union with God, because:

- Sometimes I talk to God as a friend speaks to a friend, and that's conversational prayer.

- Sometimes I memorize a prayer and repeat it over and over to discipline my mind, and that's formal prayer.

- Sometimes I talk out loud and praise His Name in word and song, and that's vocal prayer.

- Sometimes I think of an incident in the life of Jesus and imagine myself there at the time it happened, and that's mental prayer.

- Sometimes I am distraught and in such desolation of soul that I merely cry out, "God help me," and that's the prayer of anguish.

- ❧ Sometimes I am so cold and in such darkness that I merely look to Heaven and plead for light, and that's the prayer of faith.

- ❧ Sometimes I am perplexed by suffering and pain, and without comfort, and I cry out, "Thy Will be done," and that's the prayer of resignation.

- ❧ Sometimes I feel myself such a failure after so many attempts to improve, but I look to God, who alone can make me holy, and that's the prayer of humility.

- ❧ Sometimes I pray the prayers of the Church, in communion with my neighbor, and that's the prayer of the Liturgy.

- ❧ Sometimes I feel as if all is lost, but I look up to God and say, "I put my trust in You," and that's the prayer of hope.

- ❧ Sometimes I am overwhelmed with joy, and I whisper, "Thank You, God," and that's the prayer of gratitude.

- ❧ Sometimes I am aware of His Divine Presence in the depths of my soul — something unseen yet almost tangible — and that's the prayer of understanding awareness.

  And then sometimes the awareness of His Presence covers me with a mantle of serenity, and that's the prayer of loving attention.

All these kinds of prayer are enhanced by the Gift of Understanding. This gift leads me to the heights of prayer, where my soul never leaves the presence of its Beloved.

PRAYER

Holy Spirit, give me an increase of the Gift of Understanding, that I may penetrate the Mysteries of God and understand the length and breadth of His Love for me.

How I can grow in this Gift of Understanding . . .

  . . . with the Father:

I will often look at the Father and try to realize that nothing is hidden from Him, so I know He is directing everything in my life. In His Divine Light all things are visible, and He will enlighten my darkness with the light of Faith.

When doubts assail me, the meditation on the Father's love for me will quiet my soul and give me that assuring Faith so necessary to live a Christian life.

If He gave His Son for me—and He did—then He will not deny me a lesser gift. He desires me to imitate His own perfections in order to reflect His Son in my daily life.

I will take some time every day and think about His Attributes, and He will bless my efforts by giving me the light I need to penetrate these Perfections and make them my own.

. . . in the Son:

When Philip asked Jesus to show him the Father, Jesus replied, "Have I been with you all this time, Philip, and you still do not know Me? To have seen Me is to have seen the Father, so how can you say, 'Let us see the Father'?" (John 14:9).

Philip had not penetrated the Mystery of the Incarnation. He was so close to Jesus, he became so accustomed to having Jesus at his side, that it all became rather ordinary and he lost sight of Jesus as God.

I run the risk of doing the same as Philip when I lose the awesome awareness of the mystery of God and His personal love for me.

Jesus took upon Himself our human nature, and, though He was kind, compassionate, and always available, He never lost the sense of mystery that was due to His nature as God.

He took great pains to remind me over and over that He was in the Father and the Father was in Him. This, among many other revelations, He asks that I believe—if not because He revealed it, at least because of the works He performed.

Like Philip, Thomas believed Jesus was God's Son, but when it came time to accept the mystery of the Resurrection—a mystery that was not unreasonable but merely above his reason—he balked and refused to believe.

Thomas could not handle a mystery that was reasonable but unexplainable. He finally believed after Jesus manifested Himself to the Apostles.

It was then that Jesus said that all those who believed and had not seen would be blessed.

I can see now why I need the Gift of Understanding to strengthen my faith. There is a point between reason and mystery that I must both accept and pass beyond. His revelations must somehow be absorbed within me and no longer remain unrelated to my everyday life and living.

Jesus has asked me to make my home in Him (John 15:4), and the Spirit gives me the Understanding to comply with this mysterious request, by an awareness that everything I do is with Him, and for Him.

Jesus was always conscious of His Father's Presence, around Him, within Him, and in all His works.

I will follow in His Footsteps.

. . . through the Holy Spirit:

I must ask the Holy Spirit to increase my Gift of Understanding every day. I need this special aid as I read Scripture and try to comprehend the meaning behind the words I read.

When the Gift of Counsel brings to mind the life and teachings of Jesus in order to apply them to my daily life, it affects my exterior life, that is, my dealings with my neighbor.

The Gift of Understanding raises me a step higher and lets me enter into the very mystery of God, and I begin to see ever so dimly how He lives in me and I live in Him, and this affects my interior life with God.

I must read Scripture often and meditate on these mysteries that affect this interior life. The Trinity, Incarnation, Crucifixion, Resurrection, and Pentecost all affect my personal life with God, and, ultimately, affect my neighbor's life because of the good works resulting from this union with God.

This will also bear fruit in my prayer life. The more I penetrate these wonderful mysteries, the easier it will be for me to commune with God. My prayer will become more simple, quiet, and loving. It will be a total acceptance of Jesus as Lord of my life and Director of my soul.

Through the power of this Gift, my faith will be more penetrating. It will possess the assurance that comes from seeing the invisible through the light poured into my soul by the Holy Spirit.

Holy Spirit, increase within my soul the Gift of Understanding, that I may live in the brilliant light of Faith, and be transformed into Jesus.

SCRIPTURE

May the God of our Lord Jesus Christ, the Father of Glory, give you a spirit of wisdom and perception of what is revealed, to bring you to full knowledge of Him. May He enlighten the eyes of your mind so that you can see what hope His call holds for you, what rich glories He has promised the saints will inherit, and how infinitely great is the power that He has exercised for us believers. (Eph. 1:17–19)

Out of His infinite glory, may He give you the power, through His Spirit, for your hidden self to grow strong, so that Christ may live in your hearts through faith, and then, planted in love and built on love, you will, with all the saints, have strength to grasp the breadth and the length, the height and the depth, until, knowing the love of Christ, which is beyond all knowledge, you are filled with the utter fullness of God. (Eph. 3:16–19)

What we ask God is that, through perfect wisdom and spiritual understanding, you should reach the fullest knowledge of His Will. (Col. 1:9)

It is all to bind you together in love and to stir your minds, so that your understanding may come to full development, until you really know God's secret in which all the jewels of wisdom and knowledge are hidden. (Col. 2:2)

Spirit of Wisdom

- Loving as Jesus loves
- Embraces all Gifts
- Experimental Knowledge of His Presence

Much is said of Wisdom, and it is often considered an aid in times of decision.

It is more than that. When the Gift of Counsel gives me the ability to distinguish spirits, and right from wrong, through discernment, Wisdom takes me a step higher and lets me see everything as it is in the light of God.

I see with His eyes and enter into every situation with great affection and kindness.

Wisdom is the final touch in the Spirit's masterpiece. It brings all the Gifts together and cements them with love.

It is the unifying Gift that sets my complicated being on a simple and direct path to God.

Where Knowledge sees the one thing necessary, and Understanding penetrates the mystery within the mystery — Wisdom cuts through like a two-edged sword and goes directly to God; it sees God in everything and everyone without the painful effort often required in the early stages of my spiritual growth.

Wisdom gives me the ability to be at peace in the midst of turmoil, because it enables me to see the plan of God in every detail and to accept it all with love.

It is a Gift that calls forth from the depths of my soul a longing and thirst for God that only He can satisfy.

It reaches out from my being to the very heart of God, and desires a kind of union with its Beloved that no obstacle can deter.

It is ready to give and not count the cost, to love even unto death, to live and suffer rather than to die, and to count all things as loss if only it possesses the object of its love — God.

There are times when Wisdom fills my soul with deep consolations — an awareness of a Presence that only Silence can describe or comprehend; a time when God looks at me and I look at Him: no words pass my lips, but only a sense of Presence — His and mine.

But there are other times when the sense of Presence is gone, and in its place there is the Presence of Love — a giving Love — one that is content to sit and watch with Him.

This, too, is silent — silent and lonely — but Wisdom comes to my aid with the silence of faith and humility. It knows that my peace is not dependent upon feelings but upon the realization of God's personal love for me: He loves me because He is Good.

Wisdom enables me to climb the mountain unafraid, with my hand in His. I look below and often see the storms of life following, but my gaze is above — on Him.

That constant, though often distracted, gaze, is a cry of the heart, desiring the heights, falling on the way, tired of the journey but unfailingly plunging forward, where all is calm and serene.

Wisdom is:

- to keep the Commandments because I love the Father
- to love my neighbor because he is my brother
- to know right from wrong because I discern His Spirit
- to have the strength to endure because I know He did it before me
- to know the one thing necessary in this life and judge everything in that light
- to penetrate the mysteries of God with the kind of faith that moves the mountain of doubt
- to see the designs of God in my life and be content with the pattern they form
- to be calm in the midst of turmoil because I see His Providence guiding my way
- to be full of joy when I am accounted as nothing, because I live by His Word
- to be willing to sacrifice for the sake of love—God's and my neighbor's
- to count all things as nothing as long as I possess Him

Yes, Wisdom encompasses every Gift and every virtue; it knits them together with peace, and wraps them all in love.

It is the greatest of all Gifts, because it enables me to put on the mind of Christ, and then He sees with my eyes, hears with my ears, and speaks with my voice: He and I become one, and together we bear much fruit, for Wisdom brings

- Patience in suffering
- Peace in turmoil
- Joy in distress
- Love in dryness
- Self-control in temptation
- Forgiveness in injuries
- Kindness in service
- Compassion in sickness
- Resignation in death

O God, let Thy Spirit give me the Wisdom that comes from Thee — the Wisdom that encompasses all things because it is fed by love — a love like Thine: unselfish, deep, all-embracing, and never ending. I wish to be filled with Wisdom, overflowing with love, and enveloped in the tranquility of order, which is Peace.

SCRIPTURE

How rich are the depths of God—how deep His Wisdom and Knowledge—and how impossible to penetrate His motives or understand His methods! Who could ever know the mind of the Lord? Who could ever be His counselor? Who could ever give Him anything, or lend Him anything. (Rom. 11:33–35)

We are preaching a crucified Christ: to the Jews, an obstacle that they cannot get over, to the pagans, madness, but to those who have been called, whether they are Jews or Greeks, a Christ who is the Power and the Wisdom of God. For God's foolishness is wiser than human wisdom, and God's weakness is stronger than human strength. (1 Cor. 1:23–25)

We are the temples of the living God. (2 Cor. 6:16)

Now I understand how the Gifts operate in my daily life. I can see how one warns me of danger, one makes me kind; another gives me light.

Some start me off on the journey, and others lead the way.

- Both Fear of the Lord and Knowledge increase my Hope. The first gives me the hope arising from assurance; the second, a hope rooted in joy.
- Both Piety and Counsel increase my patience. The first makes me patient out of love; the second makes me patient out of merciful compassion.
- Both Fortitude and Understanding increase my Faith. The first gives me the courage to stand by Jesus; the second gives me the light to see Jesus.
- And Wisdom envelopes them all, for it makes me one with Jesus.

Litany of the Seven Gifts

When I face temptation and my strength begins to fail me . . .
   Response: *Spirit of Fear and Reverence, give me the strength not to defile Your temple.*

When my neighbor's faults and weaknesses are more than I can endure . . .
   Response: *Spirit of Piety, give me love and patience to accept all things.*

When the cross I have is more than I can bear . . .
> Response: *Spirit of Fortitude, give me courage and perseverance.*

When I am in doubt as to the right course to take . . .
> Response: *Spirit of Counsel, give me discernment and self-knowledge.*

When I put too much confidence in the things that pass . . .
> Response: *Spirit of Knowledge, give me the realization of the one thing necessary.*

When the limitations of my finite mind cause me to doubt Your revelations . . .
> Response: *Spirit of Understanding, give me light to penetrate the mystery within the Mystery.*

When Your Presence seems so far away and all is darkness . . .
> Response: *Spirit of Wisdom, let me feel His Arms around me.*

PRAYER

Lord God, I thank You for Your Spirit, whose Gifts transform me into Jesus. Bring to my mind the particular Gift I need in the various circumstances of life, that I may utilize these spiritual tools to the best advantage.

" ...the temple of God is Sacred; and you are that temple." (1 Cor. 3:17)

My Encounter with Jesus Through the Holy Spirit

Confirmed

How can I fathom the love God has for me? Was it not enough to make me a son at Baptism? The moment the Blessed Trinity made Its home in me, the Holy Spirit imprinted upon my soul an indelible sign—a seal was stamped upon me for time and eternity—in Heaven or Hell. No one can erase it or take it away. I am an adopted child of God with the right to call Him Father, and now His love raises me closer to His heart—to a union beyond my wildest dreams—another seal is imprinted upon my soul—I am an ambassador from God to the world—a defender in His Army of faithful followers—a prophet, who spreads the Good News—a member of a priestly family.

I need not envy the Apostles their Pentecost, for Confirmation is my own personal Pentecost. The Spirit has come upon me in a special way, with varied gifts and graces that enable me to imitate Jesus.

At the Incarnation, the Divine Nature and a human nature became one — Hypostatic Union — God-Man — the Word made flesh. My counterpart was Baptism, in which my human nature was raised to the dignity of a son of God — a participation in the Divine Nature. When Jesus stood in the Jordan to be baptized by John, the Spirit hovered over Him. He was anointed by the Spirit as Redeemer and Savior. He accepted His mission as the "Servant of God" prophesied in the Old Testament. "You are my Son, the Beloved," the Father said, "my favor rests on You" (Luke 3:22). And now, the Father has said the same to me! His Spirit has anointed my soul, and I am called to share the redemptive work of Jesus by witnessing to my neighbor, praying and working for his salvation, and giving him hope of greater things to come.

The seal of Confirmation has made my mission public, just as the mission of Jesus was made public at the Jordan. From that moment His dignity as Son of God, King, Priest, Redeemer, and Savior was no longer hidden. It was there for all men to see. This same Spirit has been given to me, that like Jesus, I may go out and spread the Good News of His Love and through that love change the world. O Spirit, overflow in my soul and touch all I meet. Let all men see Your special anointing in my soul. Fill me with those graces that will enable me to be always filled and led by Your inspirations. Grant that I may accept and fulfill my mission in life with a humble heart. And then, one day, when Your love calls me again and You bestow upon my soul the Light of Glory, grant that the Father may say to me, as He did to Jesus, "This is my beloved son."

Consecrated

St. Peter told the Baptized and Confirmed Christians of his day that they were "a chosen race, a royal priesthood, a consecrated nation, a people set apart to sing the praises of God" (1 Pet. 2:9).

I have been chosen by God to offer sacrifice to the Father for the sins of mankind. He has chosen me to proclaim to the world the power of His Son Jesus through the witness of a holy life. It is not a calf or bull that He asks for, but my very self—a transformation of my life—a zealous, increasing pursuit of holiness.

As the priest pronounces the sacred words of consecration over bread and wine, he says, "This is my body." I too offer that Sacred Body to the Father. The priest exercises his power by bringing down Jesus, and I exercise my priestly power by receiving that Body into my body as my own. Jesus and I become one body, and the Father accepts our joint sacrifice. Confirmation consecrates my whole being to the glory of the Father. The Father sees but one Body, with Jesus as its Head. He sees His Son continuing His Sacrifice in all the members of this Body. He sees the Spirit working unceasingly, inspiring, molding, changing, and offering these members as a pleasing sacrifice. I share in the priesthood of Jesus, and I have the right to attend each Liturgical function. The Father looks upon my prayers with love and attention. He hears my every petition for the good of my neighbor. He desires that I pray for the world and obtain for it mercy, forgiveness, hope, and love.

It is part of my priestly office to offer Jesus to the Father, praise Him for His glory, thank Him for His Goodness, and make reparation for the sins of the world.

The Father looks to me to lift up my arms in constant supplication as His servant Moses did for the chosen people.

As the tribe of Levi in the Old Testament was set apart, I too have been set apart as one to whom God has given the power to offer His Son and intercede for mankind.

It is a great dignity His love has given me. My participating in Liturgical functions is more than an obligation—it is a privilege—an appointment—a time to fulfill my priestly duty in union with the ordained priest in his ministerial role.

I confess to the world at every Mass that I am a reborn son of God. I express my love for the world by offering Jesus for its salvation. I manifest my love for the world by offering myself in union with Jesus to obtain mercy and forgiveness for my erring brother.

"We are ambassadors for Christ; it is as though God were appealing through us, and the appeal we make in Christ's name is: be reconciled to God" (2 Cor. 5:20).

Committed

"I want to urge you in the name of the Lord, not to go on living the aimless kind of life that pagans live. You must give up your old way of life; you must put aside your old self; your mind must be renewed by a spiritual revolution so you can put on the new self that has been created in God's way, in goodness and holiness of the truth" (Eph. 4:17, 22–24). I have been called by God to be "holy as He is holy" (see 1 Pet. 1:16). I cannot treat this lightly. My life should be in a continuous process of change and I should be totally committed to the Christian way of life.

The Sacrament of Confirmation has given me the right to receive from God the grace I need from moment to moment. He will never withhold that grace from me. I have a sure hope that His strength will be with me in temptation, His Wisdom when I make choices, His joy to keep me from despair, and His Providence to free me from worry.

His Spirit has given me seven Gifts — Gifts that enable me to rise to any occasion, surmount any obstacle, endure any trial. The Fear of the Lord gives me a childlike relationship with God. I can call Him my Father. Piety enables me to look upon my neighbor as a brother because we share the same Father.

Fortitude gives me the courage to withstand suffering and persecution for His sake. Counsel enlightens my mind to discern the inspirations coming from the Holy Spirit, the Enemy, or my own selfishness.

He gives me Knowledge so I can see through the folly of passing things and keep my eyes on the invisible reality. In order to feed my soul with His word, He gives me Understanding so I may pray without ceasing and trust without doubt. And then, as if to seal all these gifts so they are not lost, He gives me Wisdom, that ever-growing awareness of His Presence within me and around me.

With all these gifts and His constant attention, how can I continue living a lukewarm life or refuse to change? He only asks that I receive these gifts and use them to become holy. I am constantly exposed to His light. Why do I insist on living in darkness? He has called me to great things. Why do I hanker after petty things? I have been chosen from among thousands, yes, even millions, to be a beacon in the night—a light on top of the mountain for others to find their way.

To be a Christian is to have a special vocation. Paul told the first Christians, "Lead a life worthy of your vocation. Bear with one another charitably, in complete selflessness, gentleness and patience. Do all you can to preserve the unity of the Spirit by the peace that binds you together" (Eph. 4:1–4).

My thoughts, opinions, goals, and desires should radiate the Spirit of Jesus. I must be vigilant over my senses and ever keep His Will before me that I may "grow strong in the Lord with the strength of His power" (Eph. 6:10).

Concerned

"If our life in Christ means anything to you ... then be united in your convictions and united in your love, with a common purpose and a common mind. ... There must be no competition among you, no conceit; but everybody is to be self-effacing. Always consider the other person to be better than yourself so that nobody thinks of his own interests first but everybody thinks of other people's interests instead. In your minds you must be the same as Christ Jesus" (Phil. 2:1–5).

My Confirmation has made me a prophet of the Lord, for a prophet is one who by word and example manifests the love that God has for His people. The life of a prophet is an outward sign of the Gospel of Jesus, and so it is that St. Paul says to all Christians, "avoid anything in your everyday lives that would be unworthy of the Gospel of Christ" (Phil. 1:27).

I should have a deep concern for my neighbor, for the love of Jesus in my heart cannot be hidden. Love is a power that must go out and serve as the Master served. It was love that drove Him to work and suffer for mankind, and that same love should inspire me to have a brotherly concern for my neighbor. There are many in need whom I cannot reach, but

I must never forget that my prayers benefit every member of the human race.

I must give my love to every person who crosses my path. If he is in material need, I should help in every way possible, never forgetting that all I possess is a gift from God to be shared with my neighbor. The sick, aged, lonely, and destitute should be the special recipients of my love and care, for Jesus suffers in them.

God has set me apart as His "chosen race, His saint" (see Col. 3:12). He loves me, and my heart should be filled with "sincere compassion, in kindness and humility, gentleness and patience."

My Mother, the Church, should possess a special place in my love and prayer, for She forgives me when I sin, anoints me when I am sick, and feeds my soul with the Body and Blood of Christ. Her ministers deserve my loyalty and support, for we form one Body. I should ever uphold them in my prayers and assist them in their task as shepherds. St. Paul tells me to "Be considerate to those who are working amongst you and are above you in the Lord as your teachers. Have the greatest respect and affection for them because of their work" (1 Thess. 5:12–13).

I should strive to be "poor in spirit" so my neighbor need never feel inferior in my presence, gentle so he never feels suppressed, sympathetic so he knows I share his sorrow, merciful so he never feels I am better than he is, pure in heart so he feels loved for his own sake, peaceable so he is calmed in his turmoil, hopeful when he is discouraged, faithful in his time of need, and loving no matter how unlovable that neighbor is at the moment.

I have been called by God to do great things, the first of which is to be holy, and the second to assist my neighbor in his search for holiness. If I fail in this, all else is lost, for if I "possess all knowledge, give my body to be burned and give all I possess to the poor without love, it is nothing" (1 Cor. 13:3).

PRAYER

Holy Spirit, I place myself under your guidance. I desire to radiate the love of Jesus to my neighbor. I do not know the joys or sorrows in store for me, but I know You will temper the joys so I do not rest in them and You will lighten my burdens so I will never fall beneath them. Give me the grace to see Jesus in my neighbor and the Father's loving providence in my daily life. Let me think of my neighbor before myself and ever be faithful to Holy Mother Church. Never permit me to blur the Seal You have placed upon me.

Renewal of Confirmation

Eternal Father, all things are present to You, and so I ask that You renew all the graces and gifts You bestowed upon me on the day of my Confirmation. Let Your Spirit renew in my heart my priestly role in the Church to offer Jesus as a pleasing sacrifice, my prophetic role to be a beacon of light to the world, my intercessory role to plead for mercy, my missionary role to spread the Good News. Imprint ever more deeply that indelible seal that marks me as a son of God. Give me an increase of the Seven Gifts and let me bear all the fruits of Your Spirit. I pledge to work for Your honor and glory and for the salvation of my neighbor.

When the Enemy tempts me, the world allures me, and my own selfishness takes possession of my will, stir up within my soul that act of humility so necessary to see the grace of the moment. Ever keep my dignity as a temple of Your Spirit fresh in my mind, and never permit me to lose that sense of awesome wonder when I think of Your goodness and love. Let neither persecution dishearten me nor my own weaknesses discourage me, but renew within me a constant growth in the fruits of Your Spirit that were given me in such abundance on the day of my Confirmation. I promise, Lord Father, to listen to Your Spirit as He exercises my soul in developing His Gifts and Fruits. Fill me to overflowing with an increase of Faith, Hope, and Love so my soul may never cease giving the love of Jesus to everyone.

INVOCATION

Spirit of God, make me Patient, Courageous, Joyful, Trusting, and full of Love.

Spirit of Jesus, make me Humble, Gentle, Self-sacrificing, Obedient, and full of Faith.

Spirit of the Father, make me Compassionate, Merciful, Kind, Productive, and full of Hope.

SCRIPTURE

Your body, you know, is the temple of the Holy Spirit who is in you since you received Him from God. You are not your own property; you have been bought and paid for. That is why you should use your body for the glory of God. (1 Cor. 6:19–20)

We with our unveiled faces reflecting like mirrors the brightness of the Lord, all grow brighter and brighter as we are turned into the image we reflect; this is the work of the Lord who is Spirit. (2 Cor. 3:18)

What we ask God is that through perfect wisdom and spiritual understanding you should reach the fullest knowledge of His will so you will be able to lead the kind of life which the Lord expects of you, a life acceptable to Him in all its aspects; showing the results in all the good actions you do. (Col. 1:9–10)

Remember it is God Himself who assures us all, and you, of our standing in Christ, and has anointed us, marking us with His seal and giving us the pledge, the Spirit, that we carry in our hearts. (2 Cor. 1:21–22)

Guard against foul talk; let your words be for the improvement of others.... Otherwise you will only be grieving the Holy Spirit of God who has marked you with His seal for you to be set free when the day comes. (Eph. 4:29–30)

MASS AND THE EUCHARIST

The Mass in My Life

My Jesus, somewhere in the world Your people are celebrating the Eucharist. My heart feels cold and indifferent, and I wonder why You died for me. Was it not enough to create me to show me Your love?

The Mass proclaims Your death to the world. The world has forgotten Your sacrifice — I, too, in my lukewarmness, take Your Sacrifice for granted. This is a Celebration — a remembrance of the love You have for me and the hideousness of sin. The world looks upon sin as some minor offense — some involuntary weakness that is completely personal. How can I look upon You in Your Passion and even think for a moment that my sins are nothing? It took the Sacrifice of God's Son to atone for my sins — they deprive society of goodness and rob me of grace.

O God, forgive me my sins, but most of all forgive me for being so lukewarm — so negligent — so hardened to Your love. It is my fault, O God, my grievous faults that nailed You to the Cross.

Prepare my heart to walk with You in Your Sacrifice and permit me to unite the sacrifices of my daily life with Yours. I unite my entire life with the life You lived on earth. I desire that my moment-to-moment existence be patterned after Your perfections.

Open my ears to understand Your Word as it is proclaimed throughout the world. Your Word is like a seed, and my soul is the ground into which that seeds falls. Do not let the weeds of this world choke the seed and keep it from taking root. Let my soul be as the parched land that soaks up the living water and nourishes the seed.

My Jesus, I like to imagine You as You spoke to the crowds. I like to think my heart would have been inflamed with love as I listened to Your Word. How full of power You were as You spoke of the Father. Every word would have been so different, so gentle, and so loving. I hope I would have followed Your counsels and applied them to my life.

Why do I revel in vain desires when I can apply the words I read in Scripture and those spoken by Your priest with as much fervor now as I would have then? All things are present to You, Lord. There is no past or future — all things — every moment of time — from its beginning to its end is present to You. This being true, permit me to unite myself to every Mass being celebrated at this moment, and let me go through each moment of Your life with You. Let Your words and Your life penetrate my body and soul and make me like You.

Dear Jesus, whenever I see Your priest put wine and water in the chalice, I think of how the wine of Your Divinity was united to the water of our humanity at Your Incarnation. I unite the water of my imperfections, sins, and weaknesses to the wine of Your infinite perfections. Change me as You will change this water and wine — transform me into a clear and perfect image of all Your perfections. Let the bread of my human nature be offered with this bread on the altar, and by the power of Your

Spirit, speak the words of comfort, strength, and power that I need to overcome myself, the world, and the Enemy.

I place on the paten all my loved ones, my neighbors, poor sinners, and all mankind. I give You the people You have chosen, the priests who speak Your Word, the Church You have espoused to Yourself, and ask You to pour grace and holiness upon them all.

Do not these common items of bread and wine remind You of the nothingness from which You drew us all? But now, soon, Your power will perform an even greater miracle. It is not beyond my comprehension to understand God creating everything from nothing, but for that same God to take such simple things like bread and wine and change them into Himself is a mystery, a love that staggers the imagination and makes the very angels stand in wonderment!

Dare I offer my mite — my meager love, my tiny spark — to that flame? My God, would my spark be brighter at this moment if I forgave my brother — oh, then I do forgive — if I overcame some fault — then I shall overcome — if I were more compassionate to the weak, generous to the poor, considerate of the aged, and patient with the young — oh, then, dear God, I shall be all these things today!

Lord Father, Your divine perfections thrill my soul. You are Lord; You are Goodness itself. All creation manifests Your power, wisdom, and love. "You know me through and through." "From my mother's womb You chose me to know and love You." Everywhere I go You are there—there is no secret hiding place for me to run to. My very thoughts are known to You before they are to me. You care for me with deeper concern than a mother for her child. You provide for me with greater care than a father for his family. Your joy overflows when I reach to You in love—Your love pursues me—hounds me—when I stray from Your arms. You are glorious, and I only cry out in joyful song that You alone are Holy, Holy, Holy, Lord, God, Almighty.

Lord Jesus, Your Spouse, the Church, is in great need, and I offer Her up to You and ask that you give Her children the strength to hold fast in the face of subtle persecutions that come from the world. Give Her the zeal to proclaim the Good News to all men, the humility to trust in Your guidance through our Holy Father. Give to the faithful the grace to see Your authority behind the teachings of Your Church, the confidence to rest secure even when the Bark of Peter is tossed to and fro on a stormy sea. Guide all Bishops and Priests that they may live in Your Spirit and radiate Your life on earth.

Renew within us all a greater love for Mary our Mother, and let her example of Faith, Hope, and Love spur us on to great things. She bore You in the silence of the night, listened to Your teaching, and pondered them in her heart. She stood beneath Your Cross and watched You slowly die for love of me and then remained with the Infant Church until this new Bride was ready to follow Her Spouse without fear. Her arms were then as they are now, ever outstretched in ardent supplication for Your people. Listen to her entreaties and those of Your saints on our behalf.

I must look at these valiant heroes and follow their example. They too had weaknesses, sins, and faults, and yet they dared to scale the mountain of holiness. They kept their eyes on You, Lord Jesus, and not on themselves. Holiness seems so far off to me. You certainly died for me as You did for them. You merited holiness for me as you did for them.

Yes, my Jesus, I too am called to the heights. Do not permit me to live in the depths. Your right hand is always extended and beckoning me to go up higher — closer to the Father — above the passing things of this life. And yet I live in a material world where there is the necessity of working, eating, drinking, and sleeping — where my neighbor is in need, and society is ever running after the trinkets that glitter, and pride envelops my soul like a dead weight. But men and women whose memory I commemorate in the calendar of saints had all my problems and many more. What they did not have was my tailor-made excuses, my lukewarm devotions, and my measured zeal.

Your death and its proclamation at every Mass is enough in itself to make me holy if my faith were more living, my hope more joyful, and my love more burning.

My Jesus, I wish I had been in the Upper Room the night before You suffered for the redemption of those You loved so much. Again I entertain vain desires for am I not really present at the Last Supper at every Mass? My faith is weak and my love lukewarm. Yes, I am there — that awe-inspiring moment when Your Apostles understood Your previous revelation of Your Body and Blood as food, is totally mine at every Mass. I can offer God to God in reparation for my sins. I can receive

God into my soul so His Precious Blood, shed for me, begins to run its course in my heart.

I can see Your Face at the Last Supper, Lord Jesus, as You looked up to heaven to the Father who sent You and gave Him thanks and praise. I wish I had the courage to praise the Father before every sacrifice that His Wisdom asks of me. Give me that total consecration to the Father's Will, that union with the Father's Love.

Did the Apostles gasp in wonder as they heard You say, "Take this, all of you, and eat it: this is My Body which will be given up for you"?

I look upon the Host whenever I am at Mass, speechless and struck with awe at such humility. My life is so full of me—so full of pride—so full of the need to keep my identity. You are willing to hide Your Glory and Majesty behind this wafer, so I may gaze at my God and not die. You want me to be comfortable in Your Presence—to speak to You unencumbered by the difference in our natures. O Love that is not loved, how can I return Your love? Wash me clean, dear Jesus, clean me of every sin and weakness. Cover me over with mercy and forgiveness.

Wine is changed into Your Blood with the same ease with which Your word created light and planets, men and angels. Your word changes what was created into the Uncreated—the finite into the infinite. First, God becomes man, then God changes bread and wine into His own Body and Blood. By the separate consecration of bread and wine, the death of Jesus is proclaimed to the world. Truly I am at Calvary at every Mass for He is born, He dies, He lives, and He becomes my food.

Lamb of God, prepare my soul to receive Your Body and Blood. The next Communion I am privileged to receive must be one of great fervor, devotion, and thanksgiving. I am not worthy to receive You but that is the very reason You come into my heart. You have come to save sinners, heal broken hearts, comfort the afflicted, and console the lonely.

You are the Divine Physician who comes to heal and forgive. In Your generosity You share Your Divine nature with me, and Your Wisdom has devised such a simple way to fulfill the longings of Your heart for the love of Your unworthy child.

My Jesus, have mercy on all those among my friends, family, and relatives waiting and being purified of those imperfections that keep them from You. Release them from their place of purification and grant that they may enter Your Kingdom. If I were in their place now, I would certainly desire to have changed my life while my will had the opportunity to choose. Let me change now as I may one day wish I had done.

Grant, dear Jesus, that I may live in Your Presence, recall that Presence within and around me, and always accomplish my duties in an attitude of loving obedience to Your Will.

Our Father, Who Art in Heaven—thank You for giving me Your Son.

Hallowed Be Thy Name—give me the courage to hold Your name in reverence and never use it in vain.

Thy Kingdom Come—let all men acknowledge You as Lord in their lives.

Thy Will Be Done on Earth as It Is in Heaven—Give me the grace to live in the present moment. Let me see You, Lord Father, in everything that happens to me, in everyone who crosses my path. Let my heart ever sing one melody of union with Your Will.

Give Us This Day Our Daily Bread—Thank You for Jesus in the Eucharist, for Your food in Scripture, for Your Presence in my neighbor and in my soul, and for the bread that nourishes my body.

And Forgive Us Our Trespasses as We Forgive Those Who Trespass Against Us—O Lord, give me a merciful spirit and a forgiving heart so You may say to me at death—"I forgive you—I understand."

And Lead Us Not into Temptation—Give me the grace to prove my love for You by overcoming the world, myself, and the Enemy.

But Deliver Us from Evil—Protect me from the cunning and subtle temptations of the Enemy. Let Your angels surround me with their power and St. Michael defend me in my battles.

Lord Spirit, give me a deep realization of the Real Presence of Jesus in the Eucharist. My faith is often weak and the worries of this life rob me of spiritual realities. His humility in a tiny Host, His longing to be united to me at Holy Communion is often obscured by my lukewarmness, neglect, and preoccupation with the things of the world. I'm sorry for my tepidity and I ask You, Holy Spirit, to give me a Faith vision so I may benefit by this Gift of Gifts—the Eucharist.

Heavenly Father, when Your priest holds up the Host and says, "The Body of Christ," let my soul bow in humble adoration before the love and humility of Jesus. Let my heart be a pure resting place for Your Son. I desire, dear Father, that the image of Jesus grow brighter in my soul after every Communion. At that tremendous moment God and I are one.

My Jesus, so shine in me that together we may glorify the Father by bearing fruit in abundance. Let us go out into the world together and radiate Your love and kindness. Have mercy on poor sinners, the hungry, the poor, the sick, and the aged. Lead mankind to a deeper knowledge of Your love for them and guide us all in the right path.

My Jesus, let my heart sing out for joy, for You dwell in it. Let my mind be filled with heavenly thoughts for Your Father desires to reign there. Let my soul be guided by Your Spirit for He wishes to sanctify it.

I am a child of God through Baptism, and my resemblance to Him has grown stronger through Holy Communion. May I never forget my last Communion, and may my heart yearn for the next one.

Somewhere, someplace there is a Mass being said—a Calvary to be present at—a Communion to receive, either sacramentally or spiritually—an opportunity to be more like Jesus, the privilege of helping my neighbor, a time to say, "I thank You, God," a situation to choose Jesus over myself or a chance to make a sacrifice.

Truly, the Mass will go on and on until one day the Father will say, as His Son once said, "It is finished." Yes, the Lamb of God shall reign triumphantly with all those who have been washed clean in His Blood.

To Leave and Yet to Stay

An Oasis in the Desert

It is sad to realize that as so many believe Jesus is Present in the Blessed Sacrament, they so seldom visit Him. Men travel across the oceans to see ancient ruins, paintings, landscapes, celebrities, and mountains, but they do not think of going into a simple church around the corner to visit the Creator of all beauty.

Man complains of his tensions, hang-ups, and frustrations and for these human weaknesses he consumes bottles of pills and other remedies. He spends time and money trying to ascertain who he is and how he came to be. He is tormented by his past and entertains visions of grandeur or despair for the future.

His worries are called "mature concern," and his failures are only the result of other people's lack of cooperation. He covers up his faults and parades his least act of virtue. There are few men who know themselves and even fewer who are able to accept that knowledge with humility.

We have a need to empty ourselves, know ourselves, accept ourselves, and rise above ourselves.

We can try to fill these needs on a natural level, but when we empty ourselves, we find only a vacuum. When our weaknesses give us self-knowledge, we are saddened. When we make an effort to accept ourselves, our love turns to self-hatred, and when we try to rise above our human nature to some sublime height of tranquility, we find ourselves alone with nothingness.

We cannot purify ourselves. We cannot escape from the person we are. We cannot excuse our weaknesses. We cannot bear fruit alone and on our own power.

Our need is not so much in changing what we are, as in knowing how best to change who we are. How does darkness turn into light? How does ice turn into fire? How does a limited intelligence comprehend the mystery of life, death, and what is to come?

Where do we go to be filled, healed, forgiven, enlightened, and strengthened? Who will listen to our mumbled complaints, inner groanings, and silent doubts?

To whom shall we go when no one listens, or cares to hear our tale of woe? Who beckons to our broken heart or gives us the opportunity to cry without shame?

Who waits and waits for one thought from our cluttered minds, one whisper of love from our worldly hearts? If we do not know the answer to these questions, the fire has burned and the Light has shone in vain.

"Whoever remains in Me, with Me in him, bears fruit in plenty." These words of Jesus at the Last Supper give us a way of holiness that is both simple and easy. The Holy Eucharist is God within us and with us — it is God in us and we in God.

To maintain a close relationship with the God of Love, we must remain in that Holy Presence often. As the rays of the sun change and alter whatever they touch, so the Eternal Son, ever present in the Blessed Sacrament, changes whoever places himself in His Presence.

We must admit our weaknesses so His power can heal our wounds. We must voice our doubts so His light can dispel our darkness. We must kneel in His Presence to tell Him of our repentance.

We must silently place ourselves in His Presence, without a thought of our miseries, quietly absorbing the humility and gentleness of Jesus in this Sacrament of Love.

He is Present in the Eucharist to show us the depths of His love, the lengths He would go to be with us, the longing of His heart to be always near.

It is not important what we say in that Presence. It is only important that we are there—often—to let that Presence penetrate our souls and heal us—to shine on our minds, to strengthen our wills, to bring peace in the midst of turmoil.

His Presence in the Eucharist is silent—our presence before Him can also be silent. His Presence is humble and sacrificial, and as our faith makes us kneel before a small white Host, locked away in a tabernacle, it grows in that humble acceptance of the mysteries of God beyond our understanding. The time we give Him demands many sacrifices, but we can make them because He made the Supreme Sacrifice.

Only Jesus bears fruit in us and as we take Him into our souls as food, so we must absorb His light by sitting in His Presence—quiet in thought, loving in heart, trusting in mind.

We must be content to be near Him—to let Him work wonders in our souls—to silently absorb the beauty of His self-effacing love — to let the rays of His light penetrate our innermost being and change our stony hearts into hearts of flesh, our rudeness into kindness, our temper into gentleness.

If only we had the humility to realize that He alone is Goodness and He alone makes us good. As soon as we come into His Presence in the Eucharist, our souls respond to the power before them, like a sunflower turning toward the sun.

Before a sigh passes our lips, a thought enters our minds, or a simple word is spoken, our soul has benefited by the Presence of its Creator. Our sanctity is His work, but we cannot say yes to His commands unless His grace fills our souls and His light enlightens our minds.

If we are lonely, it is only because we have not visited our Companion in this valley of tears. If we are in doubt, it is only because we have not placed ourselves in His light.

Our weaknesses will always be with us, but we shall be strong for at least a little while, if we have spent some time in His Eucharistic Presence.

His silent Presence, hidden in the tabernacle, says to each one of us, "I love you. Come to Me, all you who labor and are burdened, and I will refresh you. Come to the fountain of life and drink. Tell Me your problems. Listen to My Voice. I tug at your heart, guiding your way and soothing your path."

Love speaks loudly in silence and that silence touches our souls. The Voice of Jesus sounds in our hearts like the voice of mighty waters, cleansing the debris collected during the storms of life. Our parched souls, tired of the journey, find refreshment in the living water flowing from the tabernacle.

There is between the Eucharistic Heart of Jesus and the soul, a silent exchange of love, a sharing of pain, an inaudible dialogue between two who know each other perfectly and love each other deeply.

It is as if the soul sees itself in a perfect Mirror and knows clearly its faults and imperfections. A strange phenomena occurs as the soul gazes at Jesus. Its own reflection becomes brighter. Its faults fade away, and one day that "soul is turned—transformed into the Image it reflected" (2 Cor. 3:18).

This being true, why do we permit our souls to die of thirst when the Fountain of Living Water is just around the corner?

Why do we live anxious, frustrated lives when the Source of Serenity waits to pour His peace into our Hearts?

Is our faith in His Presence as real as His Presence is Real, or is our faith a mere intellectual acceptance of a revelation someone told us was true? Is our Faith limited to knowledge, or is it an experience that is a Faith vision?

Do we really believe He is in the Eucharist, or do we only hope it is true? And if we do believe, why are our Churches not full, our people on fire, our spirits more zealous, and our love like God's love?

Perhaps we need to examine His Gift and see how deep our Faith really is in the depths of our hearts.

The Need

Deep in the heart of every human being there is the desire for Heaven and a fear of the death that initiates that desired goal.

It is a strange phenomenon that we cling to what is temporal, desire what is eternal, and wish that somehow we could have both at the same time.

The thought of leaving those we love in the act of death fills our souls with anticipated loneliness. We feel as if we were suddenly alone, unseen by men and unknown by God. We look at the possessions we have accumulated during the years and their value is blown out of all proportion at the realization that they will be left behind in one act of total detachment.

In this struggle we find a rich man misses his possessions more than friends, and a poor man who had no possessions regrets the loss of his opportunities. In an effort to solve this problem man tries to make a name for himself so he is remembered when death overtakes him.

The rich man builds libraries, schools, and institutions with his name in a prominent place for posterity to remember him. The poor man hopes, struggles, and prays that one of his children will rise above the depths of despair into which he was born and elevate the family name to heights of fame.

All those who live somewhere between the rich and the poor have the same fears and desires in varying degrees. So we find all mankind reaching out for a better life while clinging to a lesser life, wanting to leave this world to enjoy a better one and desiring to stay and bask in the love of dear ones.

This desire to love and to be loved, this need of the presence of loved ones is planted in the heart of every human being because we were created by the God of Love to love. When man digresses from the mission to love, he creates a Hell for himself and everyone around him.

We see this concept in the life of the Apostles. Judas refused to love. He became a misfit and finally alienated himself from Love Itself. The other Apostles with all their faults and weaknesses loved their Master and desired to grow in that love, and so they clung to Him.

Love is a flame that must be constantly fed to keep from diminishing. One of the ingredients of love is to be needed. The sinners flocked to Jesus because they had a need, while the self-complacent Pharisees were only antagonized by His Presence.

Jesus knew that when He was gone we would need a moving force to enable us to become and remain sons of the Father. He sent us His Spirit to possess our souls, enlighten our minds, direct our wills, and fill us with the virtues we need to bear the fruit of Jesus.

This He did for our sake but as God-Man — Human and Divine — Risen and Glorified — He wanted to satisfy His love for us and to feed our love for Him by a total giving.

He sent His Spirit into us at Baptism, but to complete the work He had begun He desired that He be present in our souls in a visible way.

His life on earth made Him experience what His Infinite Mind always knew: Man needs to see to believe. How could man live by Faith and yet see God? How could He leave us in order to send the Spirit and yet stay to be our Companion? How could love be satisfied and thirst satiated without interfering with man's free will and the need to choose for himself?

Would man accept a Faith vision, and would he choose Love above all things, including himself? What Divine invention would be able to satisfy all the desires of an Infinite God? Our finite, weak hearts become weary of seeking ways and means of showing love, and our minds are stunned into inertia at the thought of loving an Omnipotent God. We are only too ready to cry out, "Impossible. There is no way to love — there is no way for God and man to be one!"

Our God is inexhaustible in the ways He uses to manifest His love for us. Jesus devised a way to feed our souls, to nourish our bodies with heavenly food, to thrill our souls with the taste of Infinite Love — to stay with us after He returned to the Father.

To prepare us to accept this Mystery of Faith, He performed miracles to symbolize the reality, and then at that solemn moment before His death, He revealed just how He would be with us to the end of time. Divine Love triumphed before death paved the way for the Resurrection. He revealed to the crowds that

He would be their food and drink and told them emphatically that unless they ate His Body and drank His Blood they would not have life in them.

Before we fully appreciate this Mystery of Faith let us see how Jesus prepared His disciples for this Miracle of Love.

He Has Only to Will

It is significant to note that the first miracle Jesus performed was not a gesture of compassion for the sick or the possessed. He lived a life of work and prayer for thirty years and, as soon as He began to manifest His Divine Nature, worked a miracle symbolic of something greater to come.

He and His disciples had been invited to a wedding feast, and the wine ran out. At the request of His Mother He performed a miracle that astounded His Apostles. He asked the servants to fill water jugs with water and then merely said, "Draw out now and bring to the chief steward" (John 2:8). He did not say a prayer over the water or touch it; He merely willed that it be changed from water to wine. Only God can create or change by an act of His Will alone. He had water put into jugs and wanted wine to pour out, and it was done.

Twenty to thirty gallons of water had changed into wine because He willed it so.

Poets have said that the water blushed because it was in the presence of its Maker, but we must see more than power in this miracle. God's Prophets performed similar miracles. Elias prayed, and the oil did not diminish until the famine was over. Here Jesus does not pray as one whose gift depends upon the Will of God. No—He is God, and His Will alone creates or changes His creation.

It was so when more than four thousand followed Him and forgot to eat for three days. The Apostles had seven loaves and a few fish, and St. Matthew tells us that "Jesus took the loaves and fish, gave thanks and broke them and handed them to the disciples who gave them to the crowds" (Matt. 15:35–36).

As at the wedding feast of Cana, there was in the feeding of the multitude an important message. These kinds of miracles were performed by Jesus to impress upon the minds of the crowd that His power was the Power of God. These particular gestures of compassion were wrought as a symbol of something greater to come. Their hearts were prepared to accept a greater mystery that He would reveal before His death—the Mystery of the Eucharist. This Mystery was so great a gift from God that the human mind would never be able to accept such an influx of love without some preparation.

He would one day change bread and wine into His own Body and Blood. The same Power would multiply; the same minister would distribute from the same Source of Love — Jesus.

Although the steward at Cana and the crowds in the desert did not understand how He did it, they all realized that what He did was done out of love. He nourished their bodies, and though all benefited by the fruit of His Power, none was deprived of His personal attention and love. These two miracles foreshadowed the Eucharist.

He began His life by taking on the flesh of man and ended it by giving that flesh back to man in the form of food. He began His public life by changing water into wine and ended it by changing bread and wine into His Body and Blood.

He accomplished both miracles with great ease. On both occasions He was surrounded only by His chosen few. Both miracles were accomplished in a quiet, conversational tone of voice — as if it were nothing.

In the Wedding of Cana the only people who knew of the miracle besides the Apostles were the servants who filled the water jars with water and then watched as wine was drawn out. At the Last Supper only a few Apostles watched as Jesus said simple but powerful words over bread and wine. "This is My Body which will be given for you: do this as a memorial of Me." He did the same with the cup after supper and said, "This cup is the new covenant in My Blood which will be poured out for you" (Luke 22:19–20).

As His birth was observed by only a small group in the silence of the night, so this Divine Presence among us was given to mankind in a quiet, unassuming way. How like God to do great things with humility.

As human beings, we do great things but with the attention of the crowds upon us and all the noise necessary to keep that attention. During the temptation in the desert Jesus was asked by the devil to do three things, and all three were intended to make Jesus a performer before the crowds.

He was asked to change stones into bread. How sad that the devil has more faith in the Power of Jesus than men have. Men of today do not believe that Jesus could change bread into His Body.

The next suggestion was to throw Himself down from the parapet of the Temple. This certainly would have attracted the crowds.

The third request was absurd, but then pride is an absurdity. Jesus was asked to adore the Enemy of God for the sake of money and worldly glory. The Will of Jesus, eternally one with the Father, recoiled at the thought and told the devil to depart.

The one significant thing about the three temptations in the desert is that the real test was to see if Jesus could, by a mere act of His Will, change stones into bread, float down from the Temple parapet, and worship the Enemy. The devil knew that only God can Will something to be or to change, and it is so. Only God could change the atomic structure of one thing and make it into another by merely willing it. He waited to see the Divine Will in action.

This Act of Will was prominent in all of the healings and miracles Jesus wrought among the people. The faith required of the people made it necessary that they first believed He could heal them rather than that He would heal them.

Only once was this brought into question by one who needed healing. A boy had been brought to the Apostles by his father to be healed of demoniac epilepsy. The Apostles' power seemed suddenly limited, and the boy was not healed. The boy's father then brought his son to Jesus and said, "If You can do anything, have pity on us and help us" (Mark 9:22).

The leper who said, "Sir, if You want to, You can cure me" (Matt. 8:2) never questioned the power of Jesus, never questioned His authority. He humbly waited for Jesus to express what that Divine Will designed for him.

The man with the epileptic boy, however, questioned His Authority and Power. He brought this boy to the Apostles in the same way one goes from Doctor to Doctor. The Apostles had failed, and now he decides to try Jesus.

Jesus' feelings towards this man are very evident in the Gospel of St. Matthew. Jesus replies to the man's doubting question by saying, "Faithless and perverse generation. How much longer must I put up with you?" (Matt. 17:17).

When the Apostles saw this boy writhing and foaming at the mouth, their fear caused them to question the power Jesus had given them to heal. When they privately asked Jesus why they could not cast the demon out, Jesus told them in no uncertain terms, "Because you have little Faith" (Matt. 17:20).

A necessary ingredient of Faith then is a belief not only in what God reveals, but in His Power to accomplish anything He wills to do. Our part is to humbly wait for Him to manifest His Will. We are never sure that what we ask for is for our good, and so we wait for a confirmation if the answer is "Yes" and enlightenment if the answer is "No."

The one thing we cannot do as Christians is to question His Power and the right to manifest that Power by a mere act of His Will. God has only to Will and out of nothingness comes existence, and from existence comes change. Whether that change is abrupt and sudden or gradual and imperceptible, the same Power is at work.

It is significant of the humility of Jesus not to work miracles for the sake of show. St. Matthew tells us he did not work any miracles in Nazareth because of their lack of faith (Matt. 13:58). It says "did not," not "could not." Jesus demanded a belief in His power that was far beyond human abilities. If that belief were absent, then He would refuse to perform any miracles. They had to believe in His Divinity and Power, and submit to His Will. His humility would not be violated even for the sake of the hard-hearted.

Jesus wants our belief in His Power to do the miraculous and the impossible to be without question, and our humility to be trusting enough to realize He does only what is for our good.

When a centurion told Jesus it was not necessary for Him to travel to his home to heal his servant, Jesus was amazed at his faith. It told the crowds listening to his appeal that Jesus, being God, had only to Will—to say the word—and his servant would be healed (Matt. 8:5–13).

Jesus as Lord has only to Will, and whatever He wishes becomes a reality. Our limited intelligence cannot comprehend such a Power, and our lukewarmness cannot imagine such Love.

Why do we find the Miracle of the Eucharist difficult to accept? Is it a question of His Power or His Love? We cannot question His Power, for the One who created mountains, hills, planets, and stars out of nothing can surely change something that already exists into something else.

Neither can we question His Love. Who can fathom a Love as great as the Love of Jesus? He proved it Himself by His birth, life, death, and Resurrection. Since the source of the doubts cannot be in God, it must be in ourselves.

Perhaps we are afraid of the obligations placed upon us when we believe in His Real Presence in the Eucharist. Perhaps our love is too lukewarm to accept the total abnegation of Jesus as He places Himself into a small Host. Perhaps our pride refuses such an act of Faith—a surrender of our senses in favor of an invisible reality. How sad it is that the humility of Jesus escapes us because we desire to drag His Power down to our limitations. We must believe He is our Living Bread, our only Hope. We must trust His message and live by His Word.

Living Bread

"I am the Living Bread which has come down from Heaven. Anyone who eats this Bread will live forever; and the Bread that I shall give is My Flesh for the life of the world" (John 6:51).

In his Prologue John calls Jesus the Word. He tells us that the Word was with God and the Word was God. Jesus came down from the Father as One who gives life. All men lived in darkness, and though many saw the Light it was always at a distance — it was a Promise — a taste of something greater to come.

As men lived in the shadow of this Light they became holy, but only when Jesus became man did the Light come into their midst and live among them. Only after His Resurrection did His Spirit live within them. What they were by Promise — sons of God — they became in reality.

During their sojourn in the desert God fed the Israelites with manna. They were His chosen people, and as they wandered from place to place God kept them alive by giving them a fresh daily supply of manna.

This food kept their bodies healthy and strong, but what it symbolized increased their faith. It was a food sent by God to manifest His Providence and Love. "It was not Moses who gave you bread from heaven," Jesus told the crowds. "It is My Father who gives you bread from heaven" (John 6:32).

It is strange that in describing a past event Jesus used the present tense. The Father is still feeding His people. In the past He sent manna; in the present He sends Jesus.

The people asked for this bread of life, expecting some type of manna that would satisfy them forever. "Give us this bread always," they pleaded.

The answer they received was not what they expected. "I am the Bread of Life," He told them.

Doubts began to cloud their minds as they looked at Him and wondered what He meant. When He promised that all who went to Him would never be hungry or thirsty again, the crowd began to separate into various categories of doubt.

He tried to explain that belief in Him was a special gift from the Father and that belief and adherence to Him as Lord meant Eternal Life. They were to hear and follow the Word of God come down from Heaven.

In a very short discourse—John 6:32–58—Jesus told the crowds four times that He would raise them up on the last day; three times that He was living Bread; and twice that they would live forever. There was a condition to all these promises. This condition has two facets. "I tell you, solemnly, everybody who believes has eternal life" (John 6:47). Belief in the message Jesus gave them from the Father was food for the soul. He was man's true bread but a Bread that only Faith could receive. That Faith in Him made them heirs to the Kingdom.

He explained this kind of food when He said, "It is written in the Prophets 'They will all be taught by God' and to hear the teaching of the Father and learn from it is to come to Me" (John 6:45).

They were to hear and learn, absorb and digest the words of Jesus as they flowed from the Father. Lest they think it sufficient for them merely to hear the words, He said, "I am the bread of life. Your fathers ate manna in the desert and they are dead; but this is the bread that comes down from Heaven so that a man may eat it and not die" (John 6:49–50).

The crowd was puzzled, but before another doubt could take root in their minds Jesus explained exactly what He meant—"I am the living bread which has come down from

Heaven. Anyone who eats this bread will live forever; and the bread that I shall give is My Flesh for the life of the world" (John 6:51).

Jesus was a victim whose Body and Blood would be offered in sacrifice for the salvation of all mankind.

St. John in his Prologue tells us that the "Word was made Flesh." God became man to teach man how to be like God. Such an impossible feat needed more than a revelation to be accepted, an example to be followed. Man would have to share the Divine Nature.

For man to be a son of God, the very Spirit of God had to dwell in Him, and so Jesus promised us another Advocate. To sustain that Spirit within us it was necessary to constantly feed our souls with the Grace that the Advocate would give us.

Spiritual food was as necessary as physical food. The word of God had to be taken in by the mind so man would know what to do to please God. However, once that word entered the soul it needed power to germinate. Something else was needed to permit it to bear a hundredfold fruit. So bountiful was this fruit to become that it took over the soul completely and that soul, created with limitations, would contain within itself its very Creator. The Creator would shine forth in the soul and transform it. Love itself would take possession of the soul, and it would begin to love with God's own Love.

How was this marvel to be accomplished? Sad to say, the crowds of His time grasped the Mystery more quickly than the people of today. "The Jews started arguing with one another, 'How can this man give us His Flesh to eat?' Jesus replied: 'I tell you solemnly, if you do not eat the Flesh of the Son of Man and drink His Blood you will not have life in you.'" (John 6:52–53).

Why did the Jews not accept this statement of Jesus as a symbol? On a day in the not too distant future Jesus was to call Himself a Vine and His followers branches, growing from that Vine. They understood this as a symbol and so it was.

The Author of Truth was bound to make this Mystery clear in the minds of His listeners. Unless Truth was set forth clearly there would be no way for that Truth to be accepted or rejected. The Free Will given to man by his Creator would not be held responsible for a Light that was only faintly visible. So bright was the Light of this revelation that it carried with it the Promise of Eternal Life.

"Anyone who does eat My Flesh and drink My Blood has eternal life and I shall raise him up on the last day." Jesus used the present tense again and said, "has eternal life," and not the future tense, "will have eternal life" (John 6:40, 51).

Eternal Life begins with this Eucharistic communion of love — this intimate union of Creator and creature — this mingling of All with nothingness. The Eucharist enables Eternal Light and the created soul to join together and become one Light. Living Bread and a living soul unite and become one Love, one sacrifice for the salvation of many.

To be positive they understood what He was saying, Jesus emphasized the Mystery by saying, "For My Flesh is real food and My Blood is real drink." It appears in this chapter of St. John that Jesus is trying to explain the lengths Infinite Love will go to be loved in return.

He repeats Himself again and again as if to drive home a truth of gigantic proportions. "He who eats My Flesh and drinks My Blood lives in Me and I live in him." He wanted them to understand that two loves, one limitless and one limited, would be as one. The Flesh of the Word made Man, joining with the soul in a human being, would be so united that whoever saw the man would see the God in him.

"As I," He told them, "who am sent by the living Father, Myself draw life from the Father, so whoever eats Me will draw life from me" (John 6:57). It staggers the mind to think that Jesus loves us so much. He desires to possess us and we Him in the same way He and the Father are one. Who could ever have dreamed of such a union of love? Who could ever have imagined a Creator loving a creature so tenderly?

Realizing what was in the hearts of His listeners, Jesus tried to explain how this would be done. As if to change the subject, He said, "This is the Bread come down from Heaven; not like the bread our ancestors ate; they are dead, but anyone who eats this Bread will live forever." Only at the Last Supper would those who believed His Words then, understand how they could eat His Flesh and drink His Blood. His miraculous power would change bread into His Body.

Their lack of faith and hardness of heart worked a curious phenomenon. They missed the revelation of how He would accomplish this Mystery but they understood it was His real Flesh and Blood that they were to eat.

They took His message literally but completely missed His explanation and comparison to the manna in the desert. We have changed little since that time. We refuse to believe in a visible reality when our own minds cannot understand that reality.

We are appalled at the ignorance of men of medical science, who in the past centuries refused to believe the existence of bacteria or the necessity of cleanliness. As this is true in the field of science, it is also true in the realm of the invisible world. Lack of humility and confidence in the authority of Jesus has blinded many to the reality of spiritual truths — truths that can give us joy, peace, assurance, and eternal life.

Later, when Jesus had referred to Himself as the Vine and we as the branches, He merely stated the fact of the total dependence a creature has upon its Creator. He did not press the subject, neither did He keep repeating the simile to make His point.

Everyone present realized the symbolism of the Vine and branches, and no objections were made. This was not so in the synagogue on that memorable Sabbath when the great Mystery of the Eucharist was revealed.

"After hearing it," John records, "many of His followers said, 'This is intolerable language. How could anyone accept it?' Jesus was aware that His followers were complaining about it and said. 'Does this upset you? What if you should see the Son of Man ascend to where He was before?'" (John 6:60–62).

The important point in this incident is that Jesus knew His statement of eating His Flesh and drinking His Blood had disturbed many. The reason was obvious—they took Him literally.

At this point. Infinite Truth and Justice was bound to clarify His statement if there were any chance of misunderstanding. He told them at other times He was the Way and the Truth. His preaching would not leave a shadow of doubt in the minds of His hearers as to what He meant.

When they had not understood His message before, He took time to explain at length the meaning of His parables. Not so now. They had understood correctly. There was no need for explanations, only acceptance.

If they did not believe His gift of the Eucharist, how would they believe in His Resurrection? We find that those who did not believe the former also failed to accept the latter. The Eucharist was "intolerable" language, and the Resurrection became to them a hoax perpetrated by well-meaning disciples.

The only gleam of light Jesus shed on the subject was to tell them that "it is the spirit that gives life, the flesh has nothing to offer. The words I have spoken to you are spirit and they are life" (John 6:63).

The Father communicates life to the Son, and Jesus passes on that life to the faithful by making Himself their food. Only the Holy Spirit can give souls the light to understand this Mystery of the Eucharist. The "flesh"—the senses—human intelligence—could never invent, believe, or accept such a Mystery on its own.

Whatever is Divine can come to us only from the Spirit. To make this clear Jesus told them, "There are some of you who do not believe. This is why I told you that no one could come to Me unless the Father allows him" (John 6:64–65).

Jesus was not excusing their hardened hearts. He was telling them that because they refused to believe He was God's Son and had the power to change and transform them, the Father would not give them the gift of Faith so necessary to believe the Mystery of the Eucharist.

Faith in Jesus was the necessary quality of soul to open the heart and mind to see Jesus as Living Bread—Food for His followers to grow on and change their lives.

Their pride rebelled—first, at the thought of eating His Body and Blood; and then, at their dependence upon the gifts of the Father to understand this Mystery. "After this," Scripture says, "many of His disciples left Him and stopped going with Him" (John 6:66).

At this point Jesus looked at His disciples and said, "There are some of you who do not believe." For Jesus knew from the outset those who did not believe, and who it was that would betray Him. We seem to have three categories of doubters. First, there were those who were in the Synagogue — Sabbath worshippers. Secondly, there were disciples. Thirdly, there was one Apostle. From His most intimate friends to the average men there were those who did not believe.

Those who heard Him for the first time were the worshippers who said, "This saying is intolerable." Scripture describes the reaction of His followers by stating simply, "After this, many of His disciples left Him and stopped going with Him" (John 6:66).

Here it was that those whose enthusiasm had caused them to leave all things in the beginning, walked out on Him. Their realization that He meant exactly what He said forced them to decide whether to follow Him or not. They chose not to continue.

We find that those who had never heard Him had the opportunity to benefit by His words. They saw with their own eyes the Messiah. Their first encounter was one of shock and dismay. But Infinite Truth did not say a word to change their minds or soften their hearts.

His followers, too, those who went from town to town and city to city, watching, admiring, and cheering everything He did—those, too, had the opportunity to continue following, continue defending, but they did not, and He would not say a word to bring them back to His side.

Jesus watched the indignation of the people and the disbelief of His followers. Many walked out of the Synagogue, and in that Temple of God, God silently watched as men turned away.

Knowing the hearts of all present, Jesus turned to His Apostles and said. "What about you? Do you want to go away, too?" There must have been a time of silence before Peter said, "Lord, to whom shall we go? You have the message of Eternal Life, and we believe; we know You are the Holy One of God" (John 6:68–69).

Jesus had just told the assembly that only the Father could make them understand this Mystery. Once before when Jesus asked His Apostles who He was, Peter had said, "You are the Christ—the Son of the Living God" (Matt. 16:16). Jesus wanted all present to know how Peter knew this truth and He told him, "Simon, son of Jonah, you are a happy man! Because it was not flesh and blood that revealed this to you but My Father in Heaven" (Matt. 16:17).

By "flesh" Jesus meant our own human reason, that Intellect that is so limited in what it sees, feels, hears, and touches. Only a special light given by the Father could make one see God in a man, and see God in bread.

We can be sure that Peter did not understand exactly how it would be accomplished but He did believe Jesus to be Lord and as Lord, He could and would accomplish whatever He revealed.

This was a consolation for Jesus but perhaps it was also a source of the deepest pain. Instead of praising Peter for his witness of faith, as He previously did, He replied with a heart-rending statement, "Have I not chosen you, you Twelve? Yet, one of you is a devil." It is strange that no one asked who was possessed. Only later did they know who He meant, for John remarks, "He meant Judas, son of Simon Iscariot, since this was the man, one of the Twelve, who was going to betray Him" (John 6:70–71).

Judas was one who was more than a worshipper, more than a follower. Here was a man specially and carefully chosen to be a leader, a teacher, a witness, a friend, and a priest of the New Covenant.

For a long time Jesus was a disappointment to Judas. The cause of the Messiah seemed futile. He was not the kind of Savior Judas had in mind. His respect for Jesus waned, and he began to steal from the common fund.

With the revelation of the Holy Eucharist his disappointment turned to disgust but, unlike the Worshippers and the Followers, he decided it wiser to stay with Jesus. Was it at this time that the thought of betrayal crossed his mind? It was essential for crowds of people to acclaim Jesus for Judas to keep up his enthusiasm. When he saw them turn away, his heart sank into a state of hopelessness.

When Jesus had asked His Apostles who He was, Judas did not answer. He did not know—he did not believe. Peter, however, was open to the light of the Father. Once he believed Jesus was Lord, he could believe that Lord had power to change bread into His Body—Living Bread sent to us by the Living Father as His Living Son.

Like Peter, then, we as Christians must affirm our Faith in His Love as He gives us Himself as food, and in His Power as He changes bread and wine into His Body and Blood.

If the Voice of Jesus in the Holy Eucharist were to ask us one day, "Who do you say that I am?" may we be open enough to the Light of His Spirit to answer, "You are the Son of God."

Mystery of Faith

"I have longed to eat this Passover with you before I suffer; because I tell you, I shall not eat it again until it is fulfilled in the Kingdom of God" (Luke 22:15–16).

Jesus was not speaking of sharing a last meal with His friends. He was not very concerned about food in itself and advised His followers to use it to sustain life and not for their pleasure.

If He "longed" for this night and He did so before His death, then we realize He had some important message to give us — a message quite separate from His "suffering."

What kind of food was He to share at this meal and then not eat again until "it" was fulfilled in the Kingdom?

What kind of food would have a culmination point — a point of fulfillment? Ordinary food is digested and reaches no point of future fulfillment. What was the "it" He spoke of? These questions must be answered if we are to understand the Mystery that He offers our Faith to feed upon.

First, Jesus takes the Passover cup, gives thanks, and says simply, "Take this and share it among you, because from now on, I tell you, I shall not drink wine until the kingdom of God comes" (Luke 22:17–18).

This particular cup of wine was one of the four cups passed during the Passover Supper. Jesus had told His Apostles that He had come to fulfill the Law, and now, He executes the Law for the last time and draws a parallel between the Passover and the Eucharist He is about to institute.

After this part of the ceremony was over, Jesus "took some bread and when He had given thanks, broke it and gave it to them, saying, "This is My Body which will be given for you; DO THIS AS A MEMORIAL OF ME" (Luke 22:19, emphasis added).

Jesus, who had healed bodies and multiplied bread, took simple bread and gave thanks for it. Unlike the thanksgiving He said over the Passover wine, this time He asked for more than a sharing. This was different. The Will that created all things, willed that a change occur when He said, "This is My Body." It was the same Will that said to nothingness, "Let there be light." Just as light was made by those simple words, so bread became something greater than itself, yet retained the appearance of bread.

When the Spirit would come and take up His abode in man, man would look the same, but his invisible soul would be radically different. He would be in reality someone he did not appear to be—a son of God.

And so it was with the Bread. It seemed like bread, just as one man seemed like any other man, but that bread had changed—it was His Body, just as man was a son of God.

They both retain their own appearance, but what a change occurs! Both would take Faith to see—Faith to see God in bread and God in man.

For God to remain in man, man had to share the Nature of God. His Love would do the impossible—He would change insignificant and common bread into His Body and Blood so no one would ever be deprived of this Food.

To be assured that all mankind would possess this Food, Jesus told His Apostles, "Do this as a memorial of Me" (Luke 22:19). As He had given them power to heal bodies, He gave them power to change bread into His Body.

As once He shared with them His creative powers as they changed leprous tissue into new flesh, now, He shares something greater—He gives them power to transform and change—to say over bread, as He did, "This is My Body."

This Institution of the Holy Eucharist was done after the Passover Supper. The old was gone and the new Covenant began. Luke says, "He did the same with the cup after supper, and said, 'This cup is the New Covenant in My Blood which will be poured out for you'" (Luke 22:20).

"Drink all of you from this for this is My Blood, the Blood of the Covenant, which is to be poured out for many for the forgiveness of sins" (Matt. 26:27–28).

On Mount Sinai the blood of lambs sealed the covenant between God and His people (Exod. 24:4–8). Now, it is something greater offered to God as a covenant—a pledge of the forgiveness of sins: the very Blood of God in one supreme sacrifice pours Itself out for the Redemption of many.

Love was not satisfied with pouring out His Blood on the Cross. He desired we drink that Blood in a most palatable way. He changes wine into His Blood and that Blood gives us all the strength to seek His forgiveness, the humility to repent, and the love to change our lives to conform with the reality within us.

The Apostles were men who were given power from Jesus when He asked them to do as He had just done, to give to mankind that Sacred Body and Blood. They would ever present to the Father and to mankind the Sacrifice of Jesus on the Cross.

They would offer that one Sacrifice to God for the forgiveness of sins. Just as a mother feeds her child with the milk from her own body, so Jesus would feed those He redeemed with His own Blood.

He brought them forth from the darkness of sin into the light of the Father's forgiveness by the pain of the Cross. To be sure that His children, those whom the Father entrusted to His care, would grow into this new life of Spirit and Truth, He gave power to men to consecrate bread and wine and change them into His Body and Blood. He would continue to feed His own.

Men throughout the centuries would be privileged to kneel at His Feet on Calvary, ever present to them at the Mass, and thank Him personally for His Sacrifice, thank the Father for His gift, and thank the Spirit by whose power mere men brought down the Son of God for all to love and adore.

To the Father all things are present, and that Supreme Sacrifice of Love, ever presented to Him for the salvation of souls, brings down upon the world His Mercy and Forgiveness. It ever keeps before the eyes of our minds the cost of our Redemption and the power of His Spirit. It spurs us on to greater sacrifices, that in some small way we may unite our pain with

His pain, our suffering with His suffering, and our sacrifices with His sacrifice.

The Eucharist is truly a Mystery of Faith, an outpouring of His generosity, and a call to be holy as He is holy, to love with His own Love, for His Blood flows in our veins — His Body is bone of our bone.

He called Himself "Living Bread" because He did not will that His Supreme Sacrifice should remain in the minds of men merely as an historical event — a dead thing. No, that Sacrifice would go on as an ever "Living" Memorial of an ever present event in the mind of God.

The Eucharist in the Early Church

"These remained faithful to the teaching of the Apostles, to the brotherhood, to the breaking of bread and to the prayers.... They went as a body to the Temple every day but met in their houses for the breaking of bread" (Acts 2:42, 46).

Every day the Apostles instructed the first Christians in Holy Scripture. All the prophecies concerning Jesus were studied in the light of His life among them. Love reigned in their midst and they lived a communal life as one body of people, dedicated to the Lord. They were "brothers" of the Lord and of each other.

They were Jews who followed Jewish customs and so, after they worshipped in the Temple they went to their homes for the breaking of bread.

The "breaking of bread" was a Jewish custom. The one who presided over the meal gave thanks, broke bread, and distributed it to his family. Jesus had used this custom as part of the Institution of the Holy Eucharist.

After His Resurrection, the breaking of Bread, as the words "This is My Body" were pronounced, became a central part of their spiritual lives. The Apostles, to whom this power was given by Jesus, presided over this function as well as over the prayers said by the brethren.

Before Pentecost and many times thereafter they joined together in prayer. In the First Chapter of Acts we read that the Apostles "joined together in continuous prayer."

We get a glimpse of the functions of these men in the early Church when the social aspects of its structure began to distract them from their main duty. The Twelve called a meeting of all the faithful and told them, "It would not be right for us to neglect the Word of God so as to give out food" (Acts 6:2).

What was more important than feeding the hungry? What did these Apostles have to do that did not leave them time for this work of charity? We find that they did not neglect this duty of feeding the poor but, putting first things first, realized that as Apostles of the Word they had to take care of the spiritual food of their converts as well as their physical needs.

"You, brothers," they told the congregation, "must select from among yourselves seven men of good reputation, filled with the Spirit and Wisdom ..." (Acts 6:3).

The Apostles insisted that those chosen would be men of deep spiritual insight and not merely distributors of food packages.

The important passage in this Scripture is the reason the Apostles gave for this change. "We will hand over this duty to them, and continue to devote ourselves to prayer and to the service of the Word" (Acts 6:4).

The Apostles obviously felt their mission from God was separate from anyone else's. They were to lead the prayer at the breaking of bread, and they were responsible for the doctrinal elaboration of the Good News. Questions as to interpretation were constantly set before them. St. Peter made it clear one day when he said, "We must be most careful to remember that the interpretation of Scriptural Prophesy is never a matter for the individual" (2 Pet. 1:20).

There were times when many things regarding the sayings and counsels of Jesus were misrepresented or ill-used.

In every case recourse was made to the Apostles as men set apart in the New Covenant, as the tribe of Levi was set apart in the Old Covenant.

When Philip, the deacon, went to Samaria, he preached the Good News and "baptized both men and women" (Acts 8:12). But we find that his ministry was limited to preaching, healing, and baptizing. Scripture recounts that, "When the Apostles in Jerusalem heard that Samaria had accepted the Word of God, they sent Peter and John to them and they went down there, and prayed for the Samaritans to receive the Holy Spirit, for as yet He had not come down on any of them: they had been baptized only in the name of the Lord Jesus. Then they laid hands on them and they received the Holy Spirit" (Acts 8:14–17).

Philip the Deacon did not have the power to bring down the Holy Spirit on the new converts. It was the function of the Apostles only to lay hands on these people for them to receive this gift of the Father.

We see the Apostles preaching and explaining the Good News, breaking bread at the Lord's Supper, and conferring the Spirit by laying on of hands. They were priests of the Lord, forgiving sins in His Name, healing bodies in His Name, delivering demons in His Name, and changing bread and wine into His Body and Blood in His Name.

Faith in the Holy Eucharist was strong among the Apostles' converts. St. Paul had a special love for the Eucharist and mentioned It to the Corinthians in strong language.

Some of these Christians received the Eucharist at the breaking of bread and then proceeded to go elsewhere to eat food that had been sacrificed to idols.

Paul reminded them of their obligations when he said, "The blessing-cup that we bless is a communion with the Blood of Christ and the bread that we break is a communion with the Body of Christ" (1 Cor. 10:16). As each of them partook of the one loaf of bread changed into the Body of Christ, they formed "a single body." They were united with Jesus and each other in a way they never dreamed of.

He tried to explain that though the food they ate which had been sacrificed to idols had no value, still it constituted a communion with demons. "You cannot drink the cup of the Lord and the cup of demons," he reminded them.

The Corinthians had worshipped idols for so long that they began to combine Christianity and idolatry.

It was not long before their reverence for the Eucharist began to fall into lukewarmness. Paul was angered by their indifference and explained both the Eucharist and their punishment for receiving It unworthily.

His reprimand was in the form of an instruction. "I hear," he told them, "that when you come together as a community there are separate factions among you" (1 Cor. 11:18–19).

When they came together as a community it was for the express purpose of celebrating the "Lord's Supper." However, instead of waiting for all to arrive for this meeting, one would begin to eat his own supper while others indulged in too much drinking. "Surely you have homes for eating and drinking," Paul chided them.

The conduct of these few embarrassed the entire Community and Paul sarcastically remarked, "What am I to say to you? Congratulate you? I cannot congratulate you on this" (1 Cor. 11:22).

Paul seemed desperate to explain his viewpoint on the Eucharist, and in an effort to do so, he gives us a small glimpse into his interior life.

Jesus had appeared to Paul on numerous occasions. In fact, he tells everyone that all he learned came to him directly from Jesus, even though his humility made him check all his revelations with the Apostles in Jerusalem (Gal. 1:11–13, 18).

With this authority behind him he says, "This is what I received from the Lord and in turn passed on to you." The explanation of the Eucharist Paul was about to give had been given to him directly by Jesus. He made this point, to be sure that those who interpreted the words of Jesus at the Last Supper as symbolic would know for certain that the words Paul was about to say were the words of Jesus and not his own opinion.

"On the same night that He was betrayed, the Lord Jesus took some bread, and thanked God for it, and broke it, and He said, 'This is My Body, which is for you; do this as a memorial of Me.'

"In the same way He took the cup after supper and said, 'This cup is the New Covenant in My Blood. Whenever you drink It, do this as a memorial of Me'" (1 Cor. 11:23–25). The similarity between Luke's account and Paul's revelation is clear. Luke was Paul's traveling companion and knew him better than most. His account of the Last Supper is the most detailed, and we can be sure he and Paul discussed this Mystery often.

The Eucharist is God's new covenant with His people, and Paul tried to impress Its importance upon the minds of his converts. "Until the Lord comes, therefore," he told them, "every time you eat this Bread and drink this Cup you are proclaiming His death" (1 Cor. 11:26).

The Consecration of bread and wine into His Body and Blood proclaims to all mankind the death of Jesus. It is not another sacrifice, but the one and only Sacrifice, proclaimed anew to all the world.

Paul was not present at the Last Supper or on Calvary but as a follower of Jesus he was not deprived of this privilege. This was to Paul so real an experience that he explained, "Anyone who eats the bread or drinks the cup of the Lord unworthily will be behaving unworthily towards the Body and Blood of the Lord" (1 Cor. 11:27).

How was Paul to impress this truth upon his converts? He told them to "recollect" themselves before they partook of this Body and Blood. There was to be some time of prayer, reverence, and gratitude for such a gift from God. "Because" he solemnly remarked, "a person who eats and drinks without recognizing the Body, is eating and drinking his own condemnation. In fact, that is why many of you are weak, ill, and some of you have died" (1 Cor. 11:28–30).

Paul's faith in the Real Presence of Jesus in the Eucharist and the power of the Mass, whose Consecration produced this marvel, was so strong that he believed that all those who committed a sacrilege were punished by God.

Those who deliberately partook of this Sacrament unworthily were guilty of sacrilegious Communion, and in the mind of Paul this spiritual evil produced physical illness and even death.

This is strong language, but Paul was speaking to a hard-headed people who seemingly indulged themselves in food and drink during a Sacred function. The Breaking of Bread was no symbol to Paul but a real sacrifice and a real participation in the Body and Blood of the Lord.

As an Apostle to the Gentiles his instructions had to be clear and sound. He would not pronounce a condemnation of body and soul upon a symbol, like the Vine and Branches mentioned before.

Jesus had told him, as He did the Apostles in the Synagogue, "My Flesh is real food and My Blood is real drink" (John 6:55). It was not something to be treated lightly.

No one was to be present on Calvary eating and drinking riotously without bringing down upon himself the anger of God. "If only we recollect ourselves" he suggested, "we should not be punished like that. But when the Lord does punish us like that, it is to correct us and stop us from being condemned with the world" (1 Cor. 11:31–32).

"So, to sum up, my brothers, when you meet for the Meal, wait for one another. Anyone who is hungry should eat at home, and then your meeting will not bring your condemnation" (1 Cor. 11:33–34). Over and over, Paul warns them of the Sacredness of this Meal, this Mass. The Sacrifice of Calvary, the partaking of His Body and Blood was an awesome occasion and not one of indifference, lukewarmness, and revelry.

They had a New Covenant with God, in which He would be faithful to the end. These new converts to Christianity were to be fervent, prayerful, and zealous. The Eucharist was the very core of their spirituality. Their God fed them with His own Body and Blood. His Spirit dwelt within them, and they were in truth sons of God.

St. Paul in his Epistle to the Hebrews makes it clear that the old sacrifices were repeated over and over because "bulls' and goats' blood were useless to take away sins." Jesus, however, has offered one single Sacrifice. "By virtue of that one single offering, He has achieved the eternal perfection of all whom He is sanctifying" (Heb. 10:4, 14).

It was important for the Christian community to ever keep that Sacrifice in mind. It was to be proclaimed for all to remember. "Do not stay away from the meetings of the community," Paul urged the Hebrews, "but encourage one another to go" (Heb. 10:25).

Whatever suffering, persecution and pain they might endure, the Eucharist was their strength, their hope, and their courage. Their Jesus would be with them to the end of time.

How true were the inspired words of Malachi: "From farthest east to farthest west My Name is honored among the nations and everywhere a sacrifice of incense is offered to My Name and a pure offering" (Mal. 1:11).

God with Us

From the beginning, when man first began to live and breathe, he desired to see and communicate with God.

The Book of Genesis tells us how God fulfilled this need throughout Salvation History. God spoke to Adam in the Garden and walked with Henoch in the cool of the night.

Abraham spoke to God and heard Him promise a posterity as numerous as the stars in the universe.

Moses, in his turn, refused to lead his people to the Promised Land unless God promised to go with them. And so it was that He appeared to them in the form of fire at night and a cloud in the day (Exod. 33:13–17).

When He gave His chosen people the Commandments He requested an ark to be made, and He took up His abode among men in the Ark of the Covenant. This Presence was so awesome that when Uzzah only touched the Ark to keep it from falling, he was struck dead (2 Sam. 6:7).

After Solomon built the Temple of the Lord, we read in the Book of Kings that "when the priests came out of the sanctuary, the Cloud filled the Temple of Yahweh." "Then Solomon said, "Yahweh has chosen to dwell in the thick cloud. Yes, I have built you a dwelling, a place for you to live in forever" (1 Kings 8:10–13).

During the time of the Roman conquest, the Temple built by Herod had within it a portion called the Holy of

Holies. Here God dwelt and the High Priest offered incense to Him.

The people were at peace, knowing that God was with them. When Jesus died, however, the veil of the Temple was rent in two. It was as if God burst forth from His hiding place to rest in our hearts and in the Eucharist.

God has instilled within each of us a desire to know and see Him. Throughout Salvation History He spoke directly to some and through Prophets to others.

When the time arrived to send His Son, it was the ultimate in communication. Now, His chosen people could both see and speak to their God face-to-face.

In all past experiences of communication there was always the element of Faith. Even as men spoke to God there was never that total vision that would exclude the necessity of Faith. When Moses asked to see God's Face he was told that to see such glory meant death. Our poor human nature was not capable of such joy.

It requires humility to accept God on His terms, and so when He came in the flesh many did not believe. He preached to the poor, to those whose minds were not cluttered with intellectual speculation and whose hearts were unencumbered by possessions. In these kinds of people Faith would grow. Faith would mean an adherence to the words of Jesus as the words of the Father.

Was there anyone in Jerusalem who would not have rejoiced at the thought of speaking directly to God—face-to-face? Why was it that so many missed Him? Why did so many desire to have their God visibly in their midst and then never see Him as He walked by their side?

Jesus often reprimanded His people for their lack of Faith and He told the disciples of John the Baptist, "Happy is the man who does not lose faith in Me" (Matt. 11:6). And so it was that many found it difficult to believe that God was made Man—a man like to themselves in all things except sin.

In the beginning God had made man to His Image, but now God came down and lived in the image of man—God-Man. The miracles He performed were to prove His Divinity and Authority. To accept even these proofs demanded Faith.

No matter how much man desired to see God in this life, when he did, it took Faith to believe that the One sent by God was God—He looked and spoke like a man when in reality He was Lord of all, Creator and Incarnate Wisdom.

To those who had their own idea of how God would mani-fest Himself, Jesus was an imposter. To those who were humble of heart, He was Savior. Those who were complicated wanted a concept to ponder, a voice to hear, a revelation to decipher. Those who were poor in spirit desired God more than them-selves. They were open to Truth and ready to change their lives according to that Truth.

There was a quality of soul that all those who believed pos-sessed and that quality was Faith. Faith made them leave all things. Hope made them sure that having nothing and Jesus, was better than having everything without Him. Love made them want to be like Him, cling to His word, and one day be with Him in the Kingdom.

In order for men, outside His time in history, to persevere in this determination, they would need His Presence. They would need that invisible quality that gave mere men the power to change and follow their Lord.

The Spirit's Indwelling would give them this invisible real-ity — Grace — a Participation in the very Nature of God — God within us.

God would not only inspire men; He would dwell in their midst and through His Spirit live in their very souls as in a

Temple. This new status gave man grave responsibilities. He had to change all those temperament defects that were not in line with his new dignity as son of God.

John did not leave his converts in any doubt as to their obligations. "We can be sure that we are in God," he told his followers, "only when the one who claims to be living in Him is living the same kind of life as Christ lived" (1 John 2:5–6).

Through Sanctifying Grace man became the dwelling place of the Trinity. God took up His abode, no longer as a cloud or pillar of fire, but placed Himself in the very souls of those covered by the waters of Baptism. All those so privileged shall be as "first-born sons" in the Kingdom of Heaven (Heb. 12:23).

This grace, this life of the Trinity in the soul, had to grow and develop in a way that was a witness to the world.

There were various ways man could grow in grace. Jesus mentioned that doing the Father's Will was food for His Soul. He promised that whoever did His Father's Will was His brother, mother, and sister. All three are blood relationships.

He promised us a reward when we do the least act of kindness for our neighbor, for what we do to him we do to Jesus. The reading of Scripture, too, is food for the soul.

All these means of grace are helpful to man, but most of them depend upon our motives. Our acts of kindness are often mixed with selfish motives. Our adherence to His Will is sometimes rebellious or at least in an attitude of enduring the inevitable.

When we read His Word in Scripture our minds wander and its various interpretations escape us.

God would not leave us with various means of grace that were so dependent upon us—upon our motives—our intelligence. He knew, as Scripture reminds us, what man was made of, and He would not permit our growth in Him to be the least dependent upon ourselves.

His Grace would always be free, always be a pure gift. God's Infinite Mind devised a way to guarantee man a pure source of grace, totally independent of man's holiness or worth: a soul that could always be pure and holy as He is pure and holy, by partaking of His Body and Blood.

He devised a way by which He would be food for man's soul to grow, develop, and one day enter His own Kingdom as a son.

"He who eats My Flesh and drinks My Blood lives in Me and I live in him" (John 6:56). A real sharing of His Body and Blood enables God to live in each soul. It makes us all brothers and sisters because we share the same Father and partake of the same Body and Blood.

He knew that we would need Someone to see with our eyes and experience with our senses. We want to see, touch, and taste what our Faith tells us exists—God.

What a marvel of Wisdom! We can see Him and live in Him without any interference with the Faith so necessary in this exile.

We can see Him and not die; we can touch Him and not be annihilated. We can speak to Him in the Eucharist and have that assurance that He has heard us.

Our Faith tells us He is truly, really, and substantially present in the Eucharist.

Our Hope gives us that joy which begins here and culminates in Eternity.

Our Love is set aflame by being cast into the Fire of His Love.

This Gift of Gifts—the Eucharist—permits us to talk to God like Moses, look upon His Face like Peter, become His dwelling place like Mary, be zealous like Paul, courageous like Stephen, repentant like Magdalen, enlightened like Philip, and loving like John.

It is more than power, more than solace in the heat, or a refuge in the storm.

The Eucharist is food for starving souls, His Presence in our midst, His grace in our souls, His companionship during our journey, His strength in our weakness, the center of our lives, the yeast in the dough of our spirituality.

The Eucharist is God with us—God in us.

My Jesus, Your love for me is beyond my comprehension. I am speechless at the thought that Infinite Intelligence dwells in this Bread and Wine before me. Your humility is so great and my pride so absurd. I love You in this Host, and I thank You for stooping to this level for love of me.

What makes You so much desire to be with sinners? What makes You go to such extremes to be with us? Surely You knew, my Lord, that many would not accept Your Presence in the Eucharist. Your kind of love is different from mine. My love is easily discouraged and ready to quit at the first

sight of obstacles. Give me that same unselfish love that You have, humble Jesus.

Obedient Jesus, no matter how unworthy Your priest may be, You come to dwell in the Host in his hands when he breathes the words "This is My Body." You are content wherever he places You. You are patient no matter how alone You are in this Sacrament. You do not put up a struggle when many receive You unworthily. Teach me, dear Jesus, to be obedient to Your commands — to Your least wish — Your slightest desire. Grant that I may go where You place me, do Your will rather than my own, and wait patiently for the time of Your consolation.

Eucharistic Jesus, only a few came to visit You today. What would happen if I went to the square and shouted, "He is here — He's here — here in the Host — here on this altar." Would You cry when they all turned away? Would it all seem futile to wait so patiently for just one visit from Your creatures? Is Your humility our stumbling block? Does Your

obedience to the Father's Will strain our intelligence? Sweet Jesus, give me Faith to see and Hope to trust, and Love to stay near You, forsaken and forgotten.

Humble Jesus, grant that I may understand Your love for me in a better way. The One whom the heavens cannot contain has come down to live in this small Host. I am lukewarm but Your Love is a blazing fire. I am forgetful but You never cease to think of me. You are humility itself, and I seek only myself. You wait and wait for me to visit You in Your voluntary Prison but I am so busy with petty things. Do Angels take my place when I'm not with You? Century passes century, and still You are in this Sacrament of Love, and yet there seems to be so few who appreciate Your Sacrifice, Your Love, Your longing. Jesus, let me be a comfort to Your lonely Heart.

Lonely Jesus, is it not the essence of ingratitude for so many to believe in Your Real Presence in the Eucharist and never visit You? Does Your Heart leap for Joy when someone finally comes into Your Temple to say "Hello"? What must be

Your pain if all they do is complain of their crosses and ask for more and more things. Are there many who come just to say, "I love You, Jesus in the Sacred Host"? I praise You for Your Goodness and Love. Your Mercy has no end, but I fear lukewarmness—the kind that never asks for mercy. Please, humble Jesus, make me fervent, and grant that I may never take Your Presence for granted.

My hidden Lord, the world is in such a rush. People say they do not have time to visit You—others say You are only a symbol. Let the whole world see You hidden under this Eucharistic Species. What comfort would fill their hearts if they realized they could speak to You and You were really there to listen. Increase my Faith, too, for very often I take Your Presence for granted. During Holy Week, when Your Presence is gone from the Church, I realize how very empty everything would be without You.

Body of Christ, make me holy. Fill my weak soul with an overflowing of Grace so You and I may be as One. You have

created me for Yourself. What an act of ingratitude to keep any part of me for myself. My weakness and pride make me forget You, but Your humble Presence in the Eucharist stirs my soul to repentance. Let us be hidden together in love and union.

Humble — Jesus, my soul is often in darkness. Your Presence in my soul, as in the Host, is hidden from my eyes, but I do believe You are there. Your Presence in my neighbor is also hard to discern, and yet You have said, whatever I do to the least, I do for You. All these disguises You take on in this life demand Faith, and so, sweet Lord, I ask for more Faith. I want Your Presence in the Eucharist to be so real to me that I will receive from It the grace to see You in my neighbor, in the duties of the present moment, and in my own soul.

Eucharistic Jesus, I wish I had the talent of a poet to put in rhyme the wonders of Your Love. I wish I had the words of the Saints to tell You of my desires. I wish my mind was

not so blank and my heart so empty, so I could say all those beautiful things Your Angels must say every day. I want so much to tell the world of Your Presence here in this Host and then guide them all to Your Throne. Accept my desires, dear Jesus, for my hands are empty of good works, my mind is blank, and my soul is parched from the desert heat. Accept then my wretchedness and wrap it in Your Power and change it all in the fire of Your Love.

SENTINELS BEFORE THE BREAD OF LIFE

Sentinels in action group themselves around the Blessed Sacrament to pray, adore, praise, intercede, and obtain from the Father greater growth in the Christian way of life. Their role is one of reparation for the sins of mankind and intercession for world peace. Personal holiness, through their participation in the Sacraments, is their goal. Communal prayer in the Presence of Jesus — the true source of unity — binds the Sentinels to each other as a source of power to change the world.

Sentinels are of every age and in every walk of life. Every man, woman, and child is in need of the Presence of Jesus in their midst. The following suggestions are given so each individual, regardless of age, may participate in the glorious role of waiting upon the Lord, listening to His Words, and speaking to His Heart.

I Need You, Jesus

Two of man's basic needs are to Love and to Share. Both of these
needs are satisfied in greater or lesser degree by friendship. All
men need someone outside of family relationships to share their
joys, sorrows, complaints, fears, pain, tensions, guilt, regrets, ambitions, and all the other everyday anxieties that beset them. Man
needs someone who loves him and whom he can love in return.

Where is such a friend? Have I anyone among my acquain-
tances or friends who will consistently and patiently listen to
my tale of woe and personal joys?

Where is the friend I can constantly tell of my pain without
hearing some trite statement to indicate he has heard it before?
Where is the friend who will be with me in failure, when I am
on the receiving end and he the giving?

How many of my friends would continue loving me if they
knew my inner thoughts, secret sins, and multitudinous weaknesses? How many would forgive me more times than I could
count and then continue to love me as if I had never offended
them?

Is there anyone willing to give up a sublime existence, live
poor, and die abandoned for love of me? Is there a friend willing

to love me with an exclusive love — a love totally unselfish? Is there an honest friend, one who loves me enough to correct me and gentle enough to understand my rebellion?

Where is the person who understands my problems — understands from my point of view — and then excuses my weaknesses and makes good my mistakes?

If such a friend could be found, would I not desire that friendship? Would I not criticize the person who would refuse that friendship? Yes, I would say that person was a fool.

Is there such a friend, and is there anyone who would refuse that friendship? Do I hear You say, dear Jesus, "Have I been with You so long and you do not know Me?" (John 14:9).

My Jesus, I am like Philip for I, too, ask for Your Presence; I, too, see You every day and do not recognize You in human events and in my neighbor. In my small mind Your constant, loving Providence escapes me and I see only myself and people. Your hand guiding human events is a mystery that fills me with confusion for I do not see the good You draw out of the evil in the world.

It all seems so cold and impersonal and my soul is cramped like a pebble on the beach, ever seeking for answers, ever looking to see Your Face, ever wondering if You care.

Why is my soul so besieged by doubts, my heart filled with fear, and my mind clouded by the anxiety of living in a muddled world?

Is there any escape, dear Lord? Is there any peace, any oasis, any moment of time that has somehow been kissed by Your Serenity—a moment into which I can hide and be refreshed like the deer at running water?

Have I permitted the world, my petty ambitions and annoyances so to take possession of my soul that all the beauty of Your creation passes me by like the lightening of a spring rain?

I cannot believe You would leave me alone with no one to comfort me—no one to speak to—no one in whose presence I can cry without shame and laugh without explanations.

Is there one such friend who loves me as I am and accepts what I want to be though I fail miserably in attaining my goal? Has Your Son been sent only to live among us, die for us, and then be snatched away in a glorious Resurrection?

I know Your Spirit is within my heart, living as in a Temple. I know He guides and sanctifies and His Presence is that balm forever soothing to my soul. But I find myself longing to see Jesus, and when I feel Your Spirit tugging at my heart and spurring me on to greater things, my longing increases. I am in the midst of a paradox: I possess You, and yet my soul reaches out as if it were bereft of Your Presence. The more of Yourself You give me the more empty I feel—the more desirous I am for greater love. My soul is filled with a deep realization of how incapable I am of loving so great a God.

It is then my paradox throws me into a dilemma. Where shall I turn? To whom shall I go?

Do I hear You say, my Lord, that You have solved my dilemma? Do I see You smile and say, "Don't you know or did you forget, I have given You My Son in the Holy Eucharist? His Presence is there as truly as it was in Jerusalem. Why don't you visit Him in His lowly Prison of Love?"

Yes, my Lord, I have forgotten, or maybe I have never really been sure. So many tell me His Presence is only symbolic, and I become confused. Your Church proclaims He is there, Your Word in Scripture reveals He is there, and the holiness of men, women, and children prove He is there.

I fear, my Lord, that the pride of those who cannot accept mysteries beyond their own intellect and my own lack of Faith are the real cause of my dilemma.

You have not left me alone; it is I who refuse a friend.

You have not left me without sympathy; it is I who refuse a friend.

You have not left me comfortless; it is I who refuse Your consolation.

You have not left me destitute; it is I who refuse help.

You have not left me without courage; it is I who refuse encouragement.

Father in Heaven, why am I so stubborn, proud, and faithless? Have I relegated the Eucharistic Presence to the place of a mere devotion? Has my heart been so cold and my faith so spiritless that I put Him on a par with novenas? Why do I treat a Person as if He were a thing—a mere vehicle by which I reach You, Lord Father?

His Body, Blood, Soul, and Divinity are all wrapped up in a tiny Host so His Glory will not annihilate me, His Beauty enrapture me, His Divinity lessen my Faith. He hides Himself behind what seems to be bread so I can gain the merit of acknowledging His Presence, adoring Him as Lord, and praising Him for His Goodness.

Jesus, I'm sorry for my coldness and lack of appreciation for this great Gift. My lukewarmness has made me hard-hearted and independent. Forgive me, Jesus. You will not want for companionship again. You will not be longing to see my face and be disappointed day after day.

You and I, dear Jesus, will be friends, and I will come to visit You often, share my life with You, and bring my neighbor to this place of refuge. We shall no longer be strangers to each other. Spirit of God, help me to put my trust in the Presence of Jesus in the Eucharist, my faith in this Gift of gifts, and my love in His Eucharistic Heart.

What joy fills my heart when I realize I have Jesus always with me during my earthly pilgrimage and that one day, when the Father calls me home, the same Jesus will drop the veil of Faith and I shall see Him in all His Glory. No fear will fill my soul, for the meeting of two old friends is a joy beyond description.

Sentinel in Action

The Sentinel in Action tills the basket of his soul with the Bread of Life and like the Apostles, who distributed the five loaves and few fishes, he goes out and shares the love of Jesus and the Word of God with His neighbor. The Body and Blood of Christ is the Sentinel's source of strength, power, and zeal. Like Jesus, who gives Himself so completely, the Sentinel watches with His Master, drinks deeply of the Fountain of Living Water, prays for the world, and spreads the Good News.

PRAYER

I have come, Lord Jesus, to adore you in the Most Blessed Sacrament. My soul is parched and laden with the burdens of the journey home. I wish to feed my soul with the Living Bread of Life, to adore Your Presence in a small Host, to stand in awe at the wonder of Your love for me. Fill my soul with the gifts and fruits of Your Spirit that I may change and be born again.

(Options include: Spontaneous prayer; praise; Scripture teaching; song; meditation; Benediction and repose; Mass with Anointing of the Sick after the Gospel.)

CLOSING PRAYER

I adore You, Lord Jesus, in this Holy Sacrament. I dedicate every moment of the coming week to Your service. Give me the zeal to spread the Good News of Your love by word and deed. Let my life be a living example of the fruits of Your Spirit in our midst. Quiet the doubts that so often assail me and the fears that enfold me in their icy grip. Let the words

You spoke to the Apostles ever ring in my heart: "Peace, it is I, fear not" (Matt. 14:27).

Shut-In Sentinel Waiting on the Lord

(If possible, Shut-In Sentinel lights candle before Crucifix or picture of Sacred Heart.)

PRAYER

Lord Father, I place the pain and suffering Your Love has placed upon me as a sacrifice of praise before the lonely Jesus in so many Tabernacles around the world. I acknowledge His Real Presence in the Holy Eucharist, and I ask pardon for the neglect and lukewarmness of my brethren. Since there is no distance between Your Presence and my heart, I place my heart near Your tabernacle in every Church and render You adoration and love. Have mercy on poor sinners, save their souls from the deceits of the Enemy, enlighten their minds, and give them strength to overcome their weakness.

(If able, Shut-In reads the Gospel or says the Rosary, reads a spiritual book or novena prayers.)

CLOSING PRAYER

Jesus, my Lord, forgive the negligence of so many. They do not know You as they should. I offer Your Precious Blood in Reparation for the sins of the world. Enlighten our minds and send Your Spirit into our Hearts.

Sentinel on Guard (Teenagers)

(Sentinel genuflects on both knees in front of the tabernacle and remains kneeling for the following.)

PRAYER

I kneel before You, Lord Jesus, to comfort You in Your sorrow, to praise Your humility in this Host, and to magnify Your Holy Name.

Stand erect before Jesus, confess your faults, ask to be like Him, express all the desires of your heart. Keep nothing from Him, however small and insignificant. (Sentinel may desire to sing a song or play an instrument before the Lord.)

(Scripture Reading for 5 minutes.)

CLOSING PRAYER

My Jesus, I have fed my soul with Your Presence and Your Word. Let your grace keep me ever on guard against the Enemy. Guide me in Your ways, mold me to Your image, and let me be You to my neighbor. Have mercy on sinners and bless my family, friends, and nation. Praise Your Holy Name.

Young Sentinel (Elementary School)

(Young Sentinel stands before the tabernacle, bows profoundly, then stands erect while reciting the following.)

PRAYER

St. Michael, warrior of God, be with me as I stand before the Presence of Jesus. Let the love of Jesus fill me with wonder and give me the courage to stand up for His cause before the world.

(For at least 5 minutes the Sentinel silently talks with Jesus about studies, friends, family, games, and any other subject of interest to the Sentinel.)

CLOSING PRAYER

I praise You, Jesus, and I thank You for Your Presence in the Eucharist. You are my dearest friend and I confide to Your care my life, my family, and the whole world. You are a wonderful God, full of love and joy, and I want to be like You. Make me kind and let me be full of joy so I can change the world and make it a better place to live in. I love You, Jesus.

(Sentinel bows profoundly again, turns, and leaves.)

WHY DO YOU STAY AWAY?

If one day Jesus would speak in an audible voice from the tabernacle in some Catholic Church downtown, what would He say? Would it be a resounding thunderous voice for all to hear? Most likely it would be a Voice hardly audible because of the sorrow in His Heart and the tears in His eyes.

What kind of sorrow could make God cry? What pain so deep that His power could not, or perhaps would not, alleviate? Who is there in this whole wide world so precious to Him that His longing heart would yearn to see? Whose voice does He long to hear? Whose footsteps does He hope will one day reach His ears?

Who is this person that He looks for every moment of every day, ever searching for that familiar figure? Who indeed can that special person be?

Is it the person who excuses himself by saying, "I don't need to go to Church. I keep the Commandments (except, of course, 'Keep holy the Sabbath'). I see people going to Church every Sunday and they lie and cheat all week." How clever is this deception! It makes one feel so justified — so good without the help of God — so perfect — so content that he "is not like the rest of men." How easy it is to forget that God loves each soul as if no one else existed. He created each soul with greatest care, watches over it — hovers over it — protecting and guiding it — bringing good out of every evil that befalls it. And one day, when He calls forth that soul to see what it has done with so many gifts from so loving a God, it will be all alone before its Creator — showing what fruit it has borne with no excuses, no complaining, no arguments. God and one soul — all alone. What difference will anyone else's actions, hypocrisy, or deceit matter? That one individual soul will be looking at Jesus and realizing how very much it was loved by Him during its life on each. Will it not wish with all its soul that it had worshipped so loving a Lord? Now it realizes that going to Mass on Sundays prepares the soul for this personal encounter. The Mass does this in a quiet way as the soul listens to His Word, kneels at the foot of the Cross to be touched with a cleansing drop of His precious Blood, partaking of His Body and Blood as food for the battles of the coming week and praising His Mercy as His Blessing gives it peace. Yes, our souls are made strong Sunday after Sunday to enable them to see the Glory of His Majestic Presence at the moment of death. That moment should not find us unprepared. How important it is to attend that Sacrifice — to praise that Lord — to repent of our sins — to adore His divinity in a Host, to thank Him for His Goodness. How sad is the soul who thinks it does not need so many good things!

SCRIPTURE

If you do not eat the Flesh of the Son of Man and drink His Blood, you will not have life in you. (John 6:53)

Perhaps there is another soul Jesus is looking for. Is it the one who says he left the Church because he doesn't believe in Confession? He says he will not confess his sins to a man — to another sinner like himself. But is this true? How many people, friends and strangers, already see his sins? People he has confided in, neighbors, and relatives see his weaknesses. His family often suffers from those weaknesses. These people are supposed to forgive him "seventy times seven," but do they (Matt. 18:22)? And when they do forgive, does he ever possess that perfect peace of mind and heart that makes him feel loved again by those he has offended? Is he ever sure there are no resentments in their hearts? Do they forgive and forget? Most of all, how does he obtain strength to continue his struggle to be good? If he is not sure of the forgiveness of people whom he sees, how can he be sure of the forgiveness of the God he does not see? How much more he needs assurance from Him! How much he needs His grace to do better next time! How much he needs to hear with his physical ears that God has truly forgiven him! How much he needs the peace and joy that comes from the words, "I absolve you of all your sins." Yes, an ordained priest, with God-given power, forgives, not in his own name, but in the name of the Father, Son, and Holy Spirit.

Regardless of his sinner condition, the source of the power within him comes from outside him—directly from God, the seat of infinite mercy! The God who made us bends down to our limitations. Since we sin with our senses, mind, and heart, it is through our senses, mind, and heart that His forgiveness flows like pure fresh water. We hear the words of forgiveness, and our senses are calm. We feel clean and our hearts are strengthened, our minds are emptied of fear and resentments, and we are at peace. How wrong we are to think we do not need the outward sign of forgiveness that comes to us from God through His priest. Shall we have to say even in the light of eternity, "Truly this was God and I did not know it"?

SCRIPTURE

"As the Father sent me, so am I sending you." After saying this He breathed on them and said: "Receive the Holy Spirit. For those whose sins you forgive, they are forgiven; for those whose sins you retain they are retained." (John 20:21–23)

Who can measure the depths of the longing in the heart of Jesus as He waits for that special soul that was driven away from Him by scandal? Is this not a double pain for His Heart? Those to whom He showed special love, called to the priesthood or religious life, succumb to the world, violate their vows, disdain the spiritual life, and become engrossed in self-indulgence. A cause for scandal? Yes. A reason for scandal? No. If a soul permits the lives of others to influence his own conduct and love for God, then that soul is a "reed shaken by the wind"—the Will of that soul is as weak as the Wills of those who cause him scandal. The degree of degradation may be different, but the lukewarmness is the same. The soul succumbs to bad example as it thinks only of itself. The soul did not love God, but loved the security it found in fervent, religious men and women. When that security was gone, the soul fell apart—its crutch was taken away. It did not possess a Saving Lord, but only an idol with clay feet. This is not difficult to verify because one who really loves is not concerned with his own feelings, but only the feelings of the one he loves. When a fervent soul sees casualties in the ranks of God's Army, he bleeds for Jesus. He seeks to make it up to Him by more prayer, greater love, more appreciation for the sacraments, and a deeper spiritual life.

This soul has enough self-knowledge to realize that if it were not for God's grace he could and would do worse, under similar circumstances. Yes, when someone you love deeply is crushed under the burden of disappointment, you do not add to that burden. You do not add sorrow to sorrow, lukewarmness to lukewarmness. You strive to comfort the broken heart by companionship and love. You strive to relieve the wounded by applying the oil of prayer and the bandage of compassion. To inflict wounds upon oneself because others have fallen in battle is insanity.

Jesus has promised to be with those who love Him all the days of their lives. He does not leave us orphans. The Divine Shepherd of Souls never leaves His sheep exposed to wolves.

This is why the Mass, our source of sanctity, is totally independent of the holiness of the one who celebrates it. If a priest has the misfortune to be a source of scandal, the soul in the pew is not deprived of any grace. Jesus obeys the command of an unworthy priest and changes bread and wine into His Body and Blood. What humility and love! How sad if there is one soul missing to comfort His Bleeding Heart. Why do we inflict pain upon pain and call it just and right? Do we think the miracle of the Mass is at the mercy of men? Do we think His love for us is turned on and off by the dispositions of His creatures? His love for each soul is so great that not all the sin or sinners in the whole world can interfere with that love. Yes, He will suffer the command of a bad priest to give you His Body and Blood. He will endure the sins of a weak son to raise His Hand in absolution to forgive your sins. Why aren't you there?

SCRIPTURE

Do not speak harshly to a man older than yourself, but advise him as you would your own father; treat the younger men as brothers and older women as you would your mother. Always treat young women with propriety, as if they were sisters. (1 Tim. 5:1–2)

Is it possible that He looks for the one to whom He has given an experience of His Love—a charism—a new knowledge of Himself? How can it be that those who receive gifts forget the Giver and continue to run after more gifts? Is there a chance that those to whom He has given the wine of His consolation have become spiritual alcoholics? A harsh statement, but what can one think when those who find Jesus leave His Presence in the Eucharist, His Church, and His Sacraments to run after an emotional encounter where the cross becomes nonsense and suffering a stumbling block!

The excuse that they lack spiritual leadership and are not being fed is an insult to God. Can it be that a God who humiliates Himself to dwell in a wafer in order to be our food is not enough? Or did they lose their faith as they sang their hymns of praise to their newfound Jesus? Who can say the sacrifice of Calvary is not enough to feed our souls? Calvary is not an easy place to be, but do we not experience the Resurrection in Communion? Yes, the Mass is the realistic proclamation of His Death and Resurrection so that our daily lives may be in perfect harmony with His. No sermon, no matter how eloquent, no emotional experience, no charisma or gifts can compare with the grace we receive at one Mass or the reception of one

Communion. One indeed wonders what kind of spirit tears the soul away from Jesus, from His Mother, from His Sacraments, and from His Church? What kind of experience is worth the loss of all this?

SCRIPTURE

The time is sure to come when, far from being content with sound teaching, people will be avid for the latest novelty and collect themselves a whole series of teachers according to their own tastes and then instead of listening to the truth, they will turn to myths. (2 Tim. 4:3–4)

Of all those souls Jesus looks for, perhaps the one most difficult to reach is the one who is lukewarm. Mass is taken for granted. He is not fervent when present, and neither does his conscience bother him when he is not present. He never does anything bad enough to stir his conscience so the mercy of God is hardly sought. He never feels a vacuum in his heart that cries out to God for help. His life is full of sins of omission — the good things he never does — the faults he never overcomes. His soul is comfortable and complacent and because of this he never seeks God outside of strict obligation and that on a minimal level. Spiritual blahs are mistaken for serenity. If he were cold and hard of heart, he at least could strike a comparison between himself and God, but, as it is, his soul has no one to compare itself with. He has as much grace as he desires, with no care for an increase, no worry over a decrease. His prayers are without fervor, his repentance shallow. To him, one church is as good as another, all faiths the same, all doctrine true. In his mind all men worship the same God, so it matters little how, when, or where. Since the concept of heaven is a little sketchy and his idea of hell unsure, he strives to be neither good nor evil. We can be sure God will seek him, pursue him, and try to inspire him, but the question remains, does that soul wish to be caught by Him?

SCRIPTURE

I know all about you, how you are neither cold nor hot. I wish you were one or the other, but since you are neither, but only lukewarm, I will spit you out of my mouth.... I am the one who reproves and disciplines all those he loves: so repent in real earnest.... If one of you hears me calling and opens the door, I will come and share his meal, side by side with him. (Rev. 3:15–16, 19–20)

Why Do You Stay Away?

In drastic contrast to a lukewarm soul there is the one Jesus looks for with great yearning—the one who is separated from His Church and from His Sacraments for one reason or another. Often there is a yearning also on the part of the soul—a longing to receive the Body and Blood of Jesus, to kneel down and hear those words of absolution, but circumstances, past mistakes, and situations that cannot be changed, trap the soul in a no man's land—drifting, yearning, longing, sometimes rebellious, other times resentful. Sometimes it is only a lack of courage and trust in His Providence—a lack of determination to prefer Jesus to all things, that keeps the soul in a state of sin. What kind of benefit is comparable to the agony of mind and heart in that soul? There are other souls torn asunder by their own weaknesses and circumstances that trap them in a vicious circle. These souls must remember that although their love for God is weak, inasmuch as they have preferred themselves to Him, they still retain Faith and Hope. They must continue to pray and trust, and somehow God will help them. They can go to visit Jesus in the Blessed Sacrament present in their Churches and ask for courage to do the things that can and need to be done. Let them sit at the Throne of love and mercy and place themselves at His feet so the gap between them may

213

begin to be healed and made right. Let them kneel at Calvary during the Mass and place their broken hearts on the paten as they await the day when they too will once again be permitted to receive that Divine Body and Blood of Jesus.

SCRIPTURE

Come to me, all you who labor and are overburdened, and I will give you rest. (Matt. 11:28)

There are other souls the Heart of Jesus yearns for, and they are those whose presence is before Him every Sunday, but whose hearts are full of anger and resentment. Some of these souls want to destroy everything that was and begin anew, while others wish to stand still and never change at all. Some have lost faith and attend Mass out of human respect or to please their loved ones. Some seek to destroy truth, advocating half-truths, while others refuse new light on old truths. All in all, how many are there — just to be at the foot of the Cross? How many seek to praise and thank Him for His Eucharistic Presence? How many think of Him, love Him, and are there just for His honor and glory? How many offer themselves with Him for the salvation of their neighbor? How many say, "I love You, Jesus. I long for Your Presence in Holy Communion.

I long to be like You in my daily life. Help me, Jesus, to give myself, my talents, my time, and my love to my neighbor as You did and do in this Eucharist."

Do any of us think of the bleeding Head of Jesus as we go our own ways? Are we really working for His glory when we tear His Church asunder? Let us all unite, forget our differences, lay down our weapons, and raise our arms in prayer and supplication. Let us build the Church and not destroy it. Let us give Him the joy of seeing His children one heart and one soul.

MARRIAGE

The Living Sacrament — Matrimony

A sacrament is a visible sign of an invisible reality. Matrimony is a sacrament, and as such it is a sign to the world of the invisible God living in our midst — the living God who bears fruit in the lives of two people. They are a continual sign of His Power in the world. There is special grace and power within every couple God has joined together. Everything they do singly or together, is a living out of their sacrament. Simple things like washing dishes, running a sweeper, driving to work, struggling to make a living, budgeting a small salary to meet big expenses — yes, these and all the other facets of life together have power hidden within them to make them holy. Married life is the ground of holiness; love is the seed planted by God. Life together, with its agonies and joys, pain and sacrifices, frustrations and tensions, moments of exultation and despair, all act as the rain and sun, thunder and lightning on a young sprout.

The faults and weaknesses of each one are compensated for by each other's virtues. Each possesses what the other lacks. This results in a loving dependence on each other for spiritual growth and transformation. If a married couple can form a habit of looking at each other in a sacramental way — seeing the beauty of God in each other's souls — seeking to enhance that beauty by upbuilding each other — mutually growing in the image of Jesus — then that Sacrament of Matrimony bears the stamp of the living God.

Temperaments that could create many problems are looked upon as stepping-stones to holiness — tools in their hands that chip away selfishness, sensitivity, anger, jealousy, and greed. When personal growth in self-knowledge leads to the "putting on of Jesus" (Rom. 13:14), married life fulfills the purpose for which it was created.

When growth in the image of Jesus is the goal of a young couple, the faults and imperfections that soon begin to grind are taken in hand and used to build and not destroy. If one partner is gentle and the other hot-tempered, it is obvious that each possesses what the other needs. For example, one whose temper has a short fuse has before him a living example of the gentleness of Jesus. If that gentleness is looked upon as a fruit that is good to possess, then each partner will aid the other in their mutual ascent to God. Differences of temperament may make for incompatibility in a divorce court, but before God those differences are tools that shape and reshape each other's souls into the image of God.

Family life is the backbone of mankind, and that life is dependent upon mutual giving, sharing, and receiving from each other. It entails the proper use of each other's successes and failures for mutual upbuilding. The brick-and-mortar stage of any building is not beautiful, but without it no permanent building is possible. Pieces of wood and boxes of nails are a far cry from a beautiful finished cabinet, but those pieces of wood are the cabinet — those loose bricks, bonded together, are the building. So it is with a married couple: everyday frustrations — grinding faults, worries and tensions, success and failure all make up and build that beautiful edifice of family life and living. Though all seems fruitless and without purpose; though day-to-day endurance succeeds in tying us down to humdrum living; though boredom takes hold of our hearts with an icy hand; God's Providence counts every tear, picks up every scrap, and washes away every failure. We may think all is lost, or we have failed, but if we could see ourselves in His Eyes we would see the wisdom of His Will. If we would cooperate with Him and try to bring good out of every evil, we would be more aware of our soul changing, our faith growing stronger, our hope more secure, and our love deepening. We would see the Spirit working in every facet of life, be it ever so painful.

This Living Sacrament should be looked upon with a sense of devotion for each other and for the sacrament. Married couples should have recourse to the power of the Sacrament when difficulties arise. Every priest understands that his Ordination conferred upon him various powers to heal and be healed, to loose and to bind, to consecrate and to offer sacrifice. No matter what difficulties arise, these powers are his, and as he becomes more and more aware of these God-given powers, his Faith increases, for God is working through him. He is living the Sacrament of Ordination. Everything he does increases the image of Jesus in his soul. He is God's instrument, His ambassador to the world. It is so with Matrimony. There is hidden within this everyday living Sacrament a special power. This power enables two people to live lovingly together, to bring into this world other human beings made to God's Image. As the priest, through the power of his Ordination, offers a piece of bread and says, "This is My Body," so a married couple, through the power of their Living Sacrament, look at a child, the fruit of love, and say "This is our body—this is His Temple."

There should be in the life of every married couple a continual building of the Sacrament. Since a Sacrament brings God's Presence to us in a special way, this Presence in their Sacrament should be an ongoing living experience. They should daily place themselves in this awesome Presence by placing themselves before God in a daily encounter of love and need. If a married couple would begin their day hand in hand and silently place themselves before His Presence, become aware of that Presence around them and within them, absorb the beautiful qualities of God that they feel in need of, ask His blessing on their new day, and then make the Sign of the Cross on each other's forehead as a sign of anointing—that day would begin in His Love, and that love, stronger than death, would hold them up no matter what happened.

Prayer and the Presence of God are necessary for the fruitful living of every state in life, but how much more in those states that are themselves a Sacrament! When we begin to live in the shadow of our own presence, our world gets smaller, our views narrow, and our attitudes intensely self-centered. Everything and everyone around us jars our nerves and sets our teeth on edge. It isn't always this way because life is impossible, but because our attitudes and selfishness narrow our perspectives, and our pain is concentrated in the small area of our own private world. That intensity makes life unbearable, the future bleak, and the past a total failure. Any couple with these attitudes cannot see good in anything that happens to them, much less anything good in each other. Excuses for hatred, adultery, coldness, and indifference abound and are rationalized because the misery they feel seems so real and unavoidable. The truth is that it is real, but it is something that can be avoided and used as rungs on the ladder of holiness.

Once we realize that human frailties give us opportunities to choose between acting like ourselves or acting like Jesus in any given situation, we begin to see the necessity of responding with love instead of reacting with uncontrolled anger.

The virtues of patience, love, gentleness, fortitude, faithfulness, trust, and self-control are not easy to acquire except through the power of the Spirit living in us. These are "decision" virtues—products of our will choosing to be the opposite of any bad feeling welling up within us. When we must fight against the evil tendencies within us on a daily basis, our souls become weary of the effort, our will lags, and our determination weakens. Perseverance becomes difficult, and the reality of this struggle going on for years paralyzes our soul into spiritual inertia.

How can a soul reach for peace and joy and everything it longs to be unless that soul places itself within the Presence that ever surrounds and penetrates its being? To consistently be unaware of that Presence is to be a cube of ice in the midst of a fire. Once the soul yields itself to that Presence as one who is in need of everything, it begins to absorb the beautiful qualities of that Divine Presence. Faults, weaknesses, and temperament clashes begin to melt away. Root causes become exposed and are cut away, leaving room for new healthy growth.

In every Sacrament there is the Presence of God. This Living Sacrament of Matrimony must find its source in the fountain of Living Water, the Divine Presence, if it is to manifest that Presence to the world. A couple, in Jesus, is a real witness of the power of God in our midst. It is a concrete example of the life of the Trinity.

Like the Eternal Father, a man is the head of the family unit. He is that family's protector and provider. He has within him the seed of life. His obligations to his family require that he both give and receive. As he cooperates with the Father he exercises the power within him to bring new life into the world. He takes the spiritual elements of that life and guides it by word and deed back to the Father of all. He is to be compassionate, merciful, and understanding. The lives under his care are to be led, not pushed into the Kingdom. His protection is to be tempered by his discernment so those under his care can blossom slowly and take on the full flavor of holiness. He is to correct with gentleness, measuring punishment with the rod of compassion and not personal anger. His attitudes towards his partner should be that of a "helpmate." The book of Genesis tells us that God said it was not good for man to live alone and so He gave him a "helpmate"—someone in whom he could confide—help him make decisions—comfort him—love him and be as one with him (Gen. 2:18). There is no question of one being superior and the other inferior—it is the harmony of two individuals living as one and performing their different roles as one. These roles dovetail and are only complete when both are faithful to the part given them by the Father. These roles cannot be exchanged, because neither possesses the qualities, dispositions, power, or temperament of the other. Each possesses those special qualities given by God to perform their specific role of building each other into that one temple from which the Lord God reigns.

The woman is a gentle, loving bond who encourages, consoles, builds, reconciles, and makes all things new and vibrant. The woman is strength in time of suffering, courageous in failure, intuitive in time of danger. A woman is ingenuous when all fails, resourceful in times of want, and a true helpmate for man.

A man is strong in body, keen in mind, practical, and inventive. He is protective and comforting, full of assurance, confidence, and self-knowledge with special abilities to provide and care for his family. A man needs someone to appreciate his ability, to listen, and to hear. How lonely he would be without those special qualities his helpmate, woman, gives him.

We can see that since God has designed Matrimony as a Sacrament, those who are joined together possess unique, personal qualities that each should share and help transform to supernatural levels in each other. That invisible Presence that binds them together must become visible by their love for each other, their family life, their growth in holiness, their concern for the needs of others, their faithfulness, and their perseverance in daily good.

The Trinity that keeps their love for each other growing, begins to manifest each of the Divine Persons in the family unit. The Eternal Father is manifested in the growing qualities of compassion and mercy as man slowly absorbs the qualities of gentleness and understanding visible in the woman. Jesus is manifested in the growing qualities of humility and meekness as woman slowly absorbs the qualities of strength and self-knowledge in man. Their growing love for each other produces images of themselves in children, and this completes the family circle — the visible sign of the invisible Trinity.

The knowledge the Eternal Father has of Himself is the Son, and the love that proceeds from both is the Holy Spirit. In turn, in the family unit, man manifests the qualities of the Father and woman the qualities of Jesus. Children, proceeding from love, manifest the Spirit. Each are distinct, though all are one. Each have qualities of soul the other needs. Each share in each other's qualities, and so become more transformed into their model — the Eternal Trinity.

Though those living this Sacrament may fall short, let them always have in their mind the heights of their vocation — the call to holiness and the designs of the Father as He joined them together and made them one.

The children of such a couple become a source of love and fulfillment. They have the power to bring out of father and mother hidden qualities that would never manifest themselves without them. Parents exercise their roles in a higher degree as they form, educate, and teach their children. The compassion and understanding of the father grow in degree and quality as opportunities present themselves. A woman becomes a bond of unity and a means of reconciliation. She begins to practice those inner qualities of kindness and love never before manifested. A new spirit of sacrifice issues forth as her role in the family is enhanced. In mutually giving themselves to the fruit of their love, that love grows. Love increases when pain and sacrifice, cheerfully accepted, is borne with Faith and Hope. Any kind of selfishness that would manifest itself at this point in a couple's life would warp their marriage, decrease their love for each other, and create tension. When possessions and pleasure take the place of children, the fire of love grows cold. Love begets love, and when love is prevented from giving of itself, human nature takes over and living becomes an endurance test — a wild chase after fleeting pleasures — pleasures that merely distract from one's obligations and duties in this state of life.

Since Matrimony is a sacrament from which the couple receive the very source of love — God — it cannot be a living sacrament if love is deliberately cut off. Only the binding aspect of the sacrament remains, and such a couple soon begins to feel only the tight pressure of those indissoluble ropes. Deliberate decisions to be selfish in any state of life, be it married, single, or religious, brings havoc. Though the single life or religious life are not sacraments in themselves, those in these states receive other sacraments and the principles of living applied to Matrimony applies equally to these other states.

Our entire life was created by Love so we might choose to be love. Faith and Hope build love and if we allow those virtues to lessen by selfish choices, we remove ourselves from the source of all warmth, goodness, kindness, and joy. Instead of seeing God's hand in the present moment, we see only people and things, and Faith lessens. Instead of watching God bring good out of all our pain, frustration, and heartache, we see only evil intentions, and we lose Hope and Joy. In this type of atmosphere it is difficult, if not impossible, for love to grow.

To assure ourselves of this growth the frequent reception of the Eucharist — the Real Presence of Love — and the healing Sacrament of Reconciliation are indispensable. Without

Him we cannot ascend the heights of holiness. Without the healing balm of Absolution we cannot maintain a consistent thrust toward virtue and goodness.

If these two Sacraments, Eucharist and Reconciliation, are an integral part of the lives of a married couple, the Sacrament of Matrimony that they possess will make of them a Host—one body united to His Body—one Love united to His Love—one in mutual forgiveness as they are the recipients of His forgiveness. Their Sacrament will be living and feeding on the never-ending source of love—God.

CONFESSION

Sweeping the Temple Clean

God has created us to be holy. In our daily efforts towards that end we find within ourselves various attitudes and motives that are hindrances to arriving at that holy state.

Many Christians strive for a form of goodness that is on the border of sin and lukewarmness. They do not disobey the commandments, but neither do their lives change. Each confession is basically a repetition of every other confession. Each day's trial brings on more frustrations. Each heartache leads to new forms of bitterness.

For many Christians prayer is directed at God rather than to God. Christianity becomes solely a religion and a vehicle by which they calm their consciences or petition the Supreme Being for daily needs. There is a separation—a great gulf between themselves and God. It is almost like a great chasm over which one shouts for help in the hope that an invisible Being on the other side might be listening.

Too many of us live our entire lives in a kind of spiritual Utopia—a dream world of forgotten goals, imagined perfections, and covered-over weaknesses. We put up smoke screens for our sins and rationalize them to the point where we owe neither God nor our neighbor any sign of repentance.

God's Will becomes so obscure that a dense fog is like a clear day in comparison with what He wants and what we think He wants. At this stage we cry out for God's Will in our lives, but our preconceived ideas of God, goodness, perfection, and holiness stand between us and God like a medieval castle wall. We freeze and shiver from the cold of frustrated loneliness, searching for the warmth emanating from the fire of His loving will. Unfortunately, our lack of self-knowledge acts like a ball and chain that barely give us room to move in closer to the Fire. Our desires to be better keep us from freezing to death, but our lack of courage to see ourselves as we are, plants our roots securely in the land of unrealized goals. We stand still, afraid of who we are, desperate to be better, but petrified at the sacrifices to be made in order to become better. We are, then, pushed forward by desires and pulled backward by fears. We merely taste a few drops of living water.

Jesus promised the Samaritan woman at the well that those who drank the water He offered would never thirst again. He certainly was not speaking of the soul's thirst for God, for that is necessary to grow in His love. The thirst that would finally be satiated for the Samaritan woman was her need to know herself—to admit her guilt—to admit her personal responsibility and to repent.

When Jesus asked her to call her husband, she began with a half-truth. She admitted she had none, but never mentioned her life with a man not her husband. Neither did she tell Jesus she had been married five times. Jesus wanted to release her from that gnawing conscience that gave her no peace and that feeling of guilt that drove her from one excess to another.

The water of His grace poured into her soul, made her admit her weaknesses as Jesus proceeded to tell her all her sins. She was so relieved she ran through the town telling the people about the Man who told her everything she had ever done—forgave her sins and gave her a joy that had to be shared with everyone. She had found God—she would no longer be parched for want of the water of spiritual honesty.

Most of us have never reached that stage of integrity, clear vision, and humble discernment that would satisfy our need for repentance.

We do not possess enough of the Spirit of Jesus to keep our capacity for love and holiness continually being filled and continually growing. We know when, how, and what we do that is wrong, but we hardly ever discern why we do it. We take for granted that society, the devil, and our neighbor bear the responsibility of our actions. We then rush in to change them instead of ourselves. The result is only more frustration, for we ignore the real cause of our weaknesses, sins, and frustrations—ourselves.

We may climb on the bandwagon of social justice, but as long as we are unjust in even one area we are only beating the air.

We can cry out to do God's Will, but if we cling to our ideas and opinions as the best, we are deceiving ourselves.

We can see and abhor the sins of others and preach salvation to them, but if we do not look at the beam in our own eye, we merely reflect an image in a dirty mirror.

We are angered by disobedience but, in turn, tear down and criticize lawful authority.

We are hurt by a lack of gratitude and then arrogantly make demands on the time and talents of others as our due.

We complain of a lack of love on the part of our neighbor, but we ourselves never lift a finger to make their burdens lighter.

We lament our complexes, neuroses, and timidities, then spend hours meditating on every facet of our inner life and outside influences.

We rebel against the cross, then proceed to make it heavier by constantly measuring its length, height, depth, and weight.

Life for many of us is like a seesaw. We are always going up or down while remaining in the same place. We never tear ourselves away and go out into the unknown land of our interior to explore its depths, scale its mountains, fill in its valleys, and surmount its obstacles.

We are afraid to look at ourselves because we do not use Jesus as our measuring rod. We do not place our feet in His well-worn footprints. We prefer to ride sidesaddle through the wilderness rather than walk the narrow path that winds slowly but surely to the Father.

To know we offended God and our neighbor is the first step to self-knowledge, but it cannot end there. We should discern what defect of character or soul is the real cause of our failures. To merely seek out effects is like taking an aspirin for a headache when the cause of pain is a tumor.

We should ask ourselves why we react to various situations the way we do. Motives are an important part of our actions, and they often form the reason behind them.

To say we gave in to anger is only part of the fault, for if the anger is justified, it was no fault at all. We all possess a main root fault, and from that one weakness many shoots spring forth. When we find that main root fault we shall overcome many weaknesses in the conquering of one.

The more we read the Gospels, the more of an understanding of Jesus will we possess. With this knowledge comes the light of discernment—self-discernment—the kind that is suddenly aware of the degree of contrast between our soul and Jesus, its Model.

Jesus is not only Lord and Savior—He is our Model of Holiness—of Perfection—of action. His life and revelations tell us exactly what He expects of us.

We find Jesus more concerned over man's interior life than his exterior life. One day He asked His Apostles about their conversation as they traveled from place to place. They reluctantly told Him they were arguing about supremacy—who among them was the greatest. This was wrong, for envy had begun its ugly work among them. In asking the question, Jesus exposed the fault and in giving them the example of what they should be, He exposed their motive—the reason for their fault. He used the positive approach to expose and heal a negative effect.

He told them they were to be like children—humble, docile, gentle, loving, joyful, and ever preferring others over themselves. If they desired to lead, they were to be as one who serves. This contrast brought out to the Apostles a never-to-be-forgotten lesson in humility and love. They knew what they did; they now knew why they did it, and they understood what they should do about it.

Their self-knowledge had the three ingredients so necessary to be fruitful. Our examination of conscience should also bear these three aspects of self-knowledge. If we stop at any one of them, then our spiritual lives will continue on a seesaw.

Our Faith should be strong enough to tell us what we do that offends God so that . . .

Our Hope will be trusting enough to give us the courage to face the reason why we offend God and then . . .

Our Love will give us a deep awareness of how to be more like Jesus. Love makes like — love transforms — love changes the ugly into beautiful — love makes the weak strong.

Self-knowledge that constantly feeds our Faith — Hope — and Love — will always be fruitful — always be joyful — always be humble. But when self-knowledge creates doubts and makes us discouraged and lukewarm, then that knowledge has turned within the soul and acts like a deadly arrow — destroying and tearing apart what God has created to be whole and beautiful.

We should never be discouraged or disheartened over our weaknesses. Jesus has given us His Spirit to help us to be more like Him. He has given us His shepherds to lead us back home. He has given us the grace we need to repent, change, and become holy.

Only in heaven shall we be faultless and flawless. We must accept our sinner condition with humility and a determination never to give in to the weaknesses inherent to that condition. It is to the glory of the Father that we "bear fruit in plenty" (John 12:24). Each one of us will radiate different aspects of the Father's attributes. What is His by nature becomes ours through grace. It is important for us to know our weaknesses so we can turn them around and change them into beautiful facets of the life of Jesus.

Our examination of conscience should be honest, courageous, and humble. It must tell us what we did, why we did it, and how to change. It will do these things only when the eyes of our conscience rest on Jesus, for with that glance comes grace, and His "grace is at its best in our weakness" (2 Cor. 12:9).

May the Spirit, who made our souls His Temple, teach us how to examine our conscience, how to change, and how to pray to the Father in whose Image we were created.

Biblical Examen

Eternal Father, You have given me a memory made to Your image. Like You I can bring the past into the present moment and project the future into that same moment. However, I do not always use this faculty for Your greater honor and glory. I do not keep my storehouse of memories clean and swept of all those superfluities that clutter my mind and disturb my soul.

The dust of past hurts and the cobwebs of past disappointments make my memory like a forsaken room in a beautiful mansion — a junk room in an attic — a refuge for throwaways.

My memory seems plagued by either the miseries or the glories of the past. My imagination looks into the future and foresees the very worst in store. It paralyzes me, and I stand in the grips of an icy tomorrow.

My Father, I want to clean house today.

I desire to look into my soul and give You the only possessions that are totally mine to give—my weaknesses and sins. Yes, my Father, these alone are mine—everything else comes from Your loving Providence. Every virtue I am able to practice is the fruit of Your Presence in my soul. Every material possession, every talent is Your gift to me.

Truly, as I present myself before You, Lord God, I stand as one who has only one personal possession to offer—my sins. I will look at them in the light of the gospel and present them to You to change and transform into virtues, to heal the terrible blemishes on my soul, to pour the balm of mercy upon my deep wounds, to close forever the cuts of bitterness and to wash away the dead skin of old resentments.

Anyone who does not carry his cross and come after Me cannot be My disciple. (Luke 14:27)

Confession

My Jesus, what is a cross? Is it something laid on my shoulders by the Father's loving Hand? Is it my neighbor or society? Are my character and personality my cross? Is it the pain in my life or the disappointments? No — my Lord, these are all effects — they do not cause my cross — they do not measure its length — they do not add to its weight.

My cross, dear God, is myself! When my relationship with You is weak and my will rebellious, my relationship to my neighbor and myself is shallow and tense. There must be in my life an ever searching, reaching, longing desire to know You, love You, and serve You. Only when my eyes are riveted on Your beautiful Face can my arms reach out to touch my neighbor, comfort him in his sorrows, heal his pain, dispel his loneliness, and endure his failings.

My cross is truly heavy or light depending on how lovingly I reach up to You to embrace it and how far I reach out to my neighbor. When I rebel in either direction, my cross is heavy and unbearable. Let my soul reach to heaven and spread out to mankind in an unceasing act of love and service.

My power is at its best in weakness. (2 Cor. 12:9)

What a strange thing to say, dear Jesus. Are You saying that when the opportunity to practice virtue comes my way it is really Your power in me that makes me kind or patient or gentle? It must be so, for You have said that "without Me you can do nothing" (John 15:5).

When someone or something tries my patience, I must remember that the power to be patient comes with the occasion. It is there to use if only I will it. Truly, Lord, the greater my frustration may be at the moment, the greater Your power to transform me. The weaker I am, the more power You will have to help me. When the woman with the hemorrhage touched Your garments, You felt power leave You. Her need was great and Your power was attracted to her like a magnet. The weakest one in the crowd called forth Your power! Let Your power dwell in me, my Jesus, for I, too, am in great need.

You must know, the kingdom of God is within You — is among you. (Luke 17:21)

It is difficult for me to see You in myself, my Jesus. I am so conscious of my weaknesses, and I struggle so hard to be good. Sometimes I find it easier to see You in my neighbor, but when he hurts me, I find it almost impossible to see even the faintest reflection of You in him. Who am I to judge? I do not see his struggle—I do not see his victories. I do not see his deep repentance or contrition. Can it be, my Jesus, that all I see is myself and how he affects me? Is that the beam in my eye and the splinter in my brother's eye? It is strange that You made such a contrast. You hardly see a splinter, but a beam is very visible. Yet, You know, Jesus, that sometimes a splinter causes more pain than a large beam. Were you trying tell me that I tend to exaggerate the faults of others and then excuse my own? Help me to endure both my own and my neighbor's faults with grace and joy.

If you are bringing your offering to the altar and you remember that your brother has something against you —go and be reconciled first and then present your offering. (Matt. 5:23)

> When you stand in prayer, forgive whatever you have against anybody, so that your Father in heaven may forgive your failings too. (Mark 11:25)

Lord Father, I have failed to go to someone who offended me to see what I have done wrong. Neither do I forgive my brother his offenses against me before I offer my prayers to You. I find this very difficult. My hurt feelings rebel, and I consider this course of action beneath my dignity. Dear God, my pride astounds me! How can I be so outraged at another's offenses when I so consistently offend You? I expect Your forgiveness immediately, whenever I manage a weak act of repentance. Change my heart, Lord Father, so I will forgive first, forgive totally, forgive from the depths of my heart and forgive with love.

> If your brother does something wrong, reprove him, and if he is sorry, forgive him. And if he wrongs you seven times a day and seven times comes back to you and says, "I'm sorry," you must forgive him. (Luke 17:4)

Peter went up to him and said, "Lord, how often must I forgive my brother if he wrongs me? As often as seven times?" Jesus answered, "Not seven, I tell you, but seventy-seven times." (Matt. 18:21–22)

My Lord, I have a tendency to limit my mercy. I am often like the man in the Gospel parable who was forgiven a debt of nine million dollars and then proceeded to prosecute his neighbor who owed him fifteen. What a vast difference in debt! Why is it I find it so hard to forgive the offense of a fellow sinner — a sinner like myself, when I offend an awesome, pure, powerful, holy God and think nothing of it? I am so concerned about my honor, but so negligent about Yours. I want to be the recipient of infinite Mercy and then selfishly keep it for myself — dispensing meager amounts to others on rare occasions!

Father, forgive me for my lack of mercy and compassion and give me a forgiving spirit. Let me look upon the weaknesses of others with an eye on my own shortcomings. Let me reach out in understanding, gentle love, and prompt forgiveness. Wipe away the memory of every offense and replace it with a generous portion of self-knowledge so I may be humble of heart, ever realizing that without Your grace, I would be capable of any sin.

> Be compassionate as Your Father is compassionate. Do
> not judge, and you will not be judged; do not condemn
> and you will not be condemned yourself. (Luke 6:36–37)

My Jesus, I am not as compassionate as I should be. I rebel
when my time is infringed upon by the spiritual, physical, or
material needs of others. I tend to give them some trite advice,
condescending aid, and abrupt counseling. I do not want to
share their crosses because it somehow makes my cross heavier.
As I advise them to carry their cross for love of You, dear Jesus,
what I am really saying is, "I've heard enough. I can't help you,
so bear it quietly."

By not being compassionate I have set myself up as judge. I
judge the degree of pain they have, the weight of their crosses,
the motives behind their complaints, and their conformity to
Your Will. It is only a matter of time before I condemn them as
cowardly or chronic complainers, neurotic or just plain grum-
blers. I do the same with their sins. They are all neatly placed
in categories, condemned and judged as wanting in strength. I
am scandalized, and then I proceed to push both sin and sinners
aside as beneath my dignity and unworthy of my friendship.

Confession

How unlike You I am, my Jesus. You hated sin, but loved the sinner. Teach me to be understanding and compassionate, firm and uncompromising towards sin and sinful occasions but gentle and forgiving with all those who fall. Let me lift them up to new heights of repentance and great desires for holiness.

Why do you call me, "Lord, Lord" and not do what I say? (Luke 6:46)

Yes, my Lord, I am guilty of this accusation. You have given me life, a Christian home, a vocation to witness to the world, and opportunities to imitate You in my daily life. Every moment new grace is given me by Your Spirit, and I do not cooperate. I go through life, thinking only of myself and my plans — frustrated over past failures and worried about tomorrow. I live in a world that denies Your Sovereignty, and I do not challenge that stand by a virtuous life. Truly, there is a vast difference between what I believe and the way I act. Since actions speak louder than words, grant me the courage to fight for Your principles with the roar of a lion and not the purr of a kitten. I desire that my everyday life, in my particular state, be a witness to everyone I meet that You, Lord Jesus, are my guiding light, my morning star, my dearest friend, and the Master whom I serve.

Anyone who does not take his cross and follow in My footsteps is not worthy of Me. (Matt. 10:38)

I shiver when I read that statement, my Jesus. My weaknesses seem so great, my desire to do my own will so determined. Perhaps I am trying to make my own way perfect. To follow You I need only imitate Your example. I need not make a path of my own. I need not take that burden on my shoulders. My Jesus, will You walk beside me as I feebly make my way in the path You have made? Will You take my hand in Yours and hold it tightly as I waver and stumble forward? Will You prod me on as I so often look behind?

Give me a glimpse of the journey's end so I do not become discouraged on the way. Grant that my feet may ever feel the warmth of the blood trickling from Your wounds. Let that Precious Blood, given to me so generously in the Eucharist, revitalize my whole being, set me firmly on the right path, and keep my eyes ever on You.

Do not suppose that I have come to bring peace to the earth: it is not peace I have come to bring, but a sword. (Matt. 10:34)

You did not come to provoke dissension, my Jesus, but trying to think and act like You means self-denial, the loss of friends and sometimes family and home. The world is like a magnet that pulls me here and there. One day You said that only the violent could carry away the kingdom. That personal war ever raging in my soul is only conquered by the violence of self-control, gentleness, patience, temperance, and goodness. Help me to make war on myself that I may bring peace to others.

Do not worry about tomorrow: tomorrow will take care of itself. Each day has enough trouble of its own. (Matt. 6:34)

My Jesus, give the grace to live in the present moment. My pride prevents me from trusting my tomorrow to Your loving Providence. Worry is so useless, and yet my soul is beset by that frustrating rehearsal of what sorrows and disappointments will be my portion in the future. How cowardly of me to think that the Creator of the universe cannot take care of my tomorrows or the problems in my life! I lack trust because I lack love. My love is based on selfish motives, and so I attribute that kind of love to You. How unjust I am to an All-Holy and Just God! Your goodness is beyond my wildest concepts of generosity, and yet my pride gives me the illusion that my moment-to-moment existence is completely in my hands. Forgive my lack of hope, my Jesus. Instill within my soul a childlike trust in Your paternal care and guidance. Most of all, give me a deep realization of Your love for me so I can joyfully place my past in Your Mercy and never feel guilty again. Let me place my tomorrow in Your care so I may understand nothing will ever happen to me that is not for my good.

Can you not buy two sparrows for a penny? And yet not one falls to the ground without Your Father knowing. Why, every hair on your head has been counted. So there is no need to be afraid; you are worth more than hundreds of sparrows. (Matt. 10:29–31)

Confession

My Jesus, it is hard for my small mind to comprehend Your love for me. You are telling me in this passage that I am worth something — I am really precious in Your sight — I am worth more to You than hundreds of sparrows. Your Providence is so caring that every hair I flick from my shoulder without notice is seen and counted by You — counted as if it were part of some treasure. If this is true of a passing thing like hair, how much more care do You take of my soul — that part of me made to Your image! You count every pain, weigh every cross, cushion every fall, cover over my failures, and clear the path for my footsteps. You are a loving Lord — caring, protective, merciful, provident, gracious, and kind. Grant that my soul may ever keep its faculties open to the light of Your love, the warmth of Your goodness, and the power of Your grace.

Anyone who does the will of God, that person is my brother and sister and mother. (Mark 3:35)

It all seems so simple, my Lord, doing Your Will. The reward of a family relationship as compared to a servant relationship is certainly worth the effort. But even this great benefit does not move me to do Your Will rather than my own. I find excuses as though I did not know Your Will, but then there are the commandments, which shatter that false reasoning. Again I say that modern-day living makes Your Will more obscure, but I have Your Church speaking loud and clear in its teachings, dogmas, and precepts. In a last-ditch effort to excuse myself I say I do not know Your Will in everyday circumstances, but You have given me a conscience that stirs and rebels when our two wills come near the separation point. I must confess, my Jesus, that I have no legitimate excuse for not doing Your Will. My pride makes me think my way is better, my opinion more reasonable, and my plans more wise. Is my foolishness the reason Your justice does not annihilate me for living such a lie? If my present moment is proving the absurdity of pride, let my future prove the truthfulness of humility. Your Will is always perfect, always designed for my good, always rewarding and always good. Let my soul rest secure in that Holy Will. May I develop the peace of the children of God — the freedom of those whose lives breathe in the Will of their Father and exhale the sweet odor of holiness.

Love your enemies, do good to those who hate you,
bless those who curse you, pray for those who treat you
badly. (Luke 6:27)

How can I love someone who hates me, Jesus? How can I love
without a return of love? Isn't this beyond my nature? Aren't
you asking more than I can do? Only God could ask me to do
such a thing because I need some special quality outside myself
to enable me to love those who hurt me. Give me that quality—that attitude, dear Jesus. Let me see the opportunity to
be supernatural in a situation in which my nature rebels and I
want to lash out in reprisal, hatred, and resentment. Let Your
gentleness fall over me like a cloak, Your patience surround my
rebellion like a shield, and Your love cut through the bitterness
of my heart to sweeten my spirit.

And they brought Him a deaf man who had an impedi-
ment in his speech and they asked Him to lay His hand
on him. . . . He took him aside . . . put His finger into the

man's ear ... then looking up to heaven sighed and said, "Ephphatha," that is, "Be opened." (Mark 7:32–34)

My Jesus, I have ears, but they are so often closed to Your Words — to Your Will. Open my ears to hear the Father's love manifested in everything around me. Let me praise Him as I hear the silent breeze swaying the leaves on a giant oak. Let me hear the mighty power of His Majesty in the rolling thunder. Let me hear innocence in the voice of a child and wisdom in the crackly voice of the aged. Let me keep my ears open to the good sounds in life and close them tight to the noisy spirit of the world, the temptations of the Enemy, and the sound of my own selfish voice as it demands the things that are not Your Will. Say to me, my Jesus, "Be open to the life-giving Word of My Father — Be open to the inspirations of My Spirit — Be open to change, be open to a new life."

Now one day when He was praying alone in the presence of His disciples He put this question to them, "Who do the crowds say that I am?" (Luke 9:18)

My Jesus, I wonder if I would have replied with Peter, "Thou art the Christ" (Luke 9:19). Would I have seen Divinity in humanity? I do believe, my Jesus, but my life does not always witness to that belief. If my Faith were stronger, my life would be so different. I would desire to be more like You in my everyday life. I would be more determined to change those traits in my personality that annoy my neighbor. I would look forward to the Kingdom and see the things of this world in the right light. I would be filled with a joy so deep that neither pain nor trials could destroy. I would have peace in the midst of turmoil if my Faith took up its residence in my heart as well as my mind. Give me the Faith that moves the mountains of my lethargy, and give me zeal to work tirelessly for the spread of the Good News You came to give us. Let me be courageous enough to say to the whole world, "Jesus is Lord, the Son of God, the Savior of all mankind."

Ask, and it will be given to you; search, and you will find; knock and the door will be opened to you. (Matt. 7:7)

My Jesus, I get very discouraged in prayer. It seems the more I pray for something, the further away it goes. I fail to ask and seek and knock. I do not persevere. I am not persistent. My Faith is weak and I feel You do not hear my voice, or worse, You do not care. I am so sure that what I desire is for my good, I lose confidence in Your Wisdom and complain of unanswered prayers. Help me to realize, my Lord, that persevering prayer with a loving heart and a faith-filled mind will always give me confidence in Your concern. I will know, without hesitation in my heart, that every prayer is answered by an all-wise God. I will have the assurance and hope that rests secure in a "no" answer as well as a "yes" because Your love follows me and Your providence goes ahead of me. No matter what befalls me, You are there before I arrive, ready to help, console, and protect me. My Lord, help me to pray without ceasing, love without limit, and trust without doubt.

Blessed are the poor in spirit. (Matt. 5:3)
My Jesus, I am rich in spirit—I am not content with You alone. I am not detached from the things of this world. Give

me an affectionate heart that I may love with detachment and freedom.

Blessed the gentle. (Matt. 5:5)
Teach me how to be gentle, my Jesus. Anger is often the order of the day, and I fail to see strength in gentleness. Give me self-control that my neighbor does not suffer from my lack of virtue.

Blessed those who mourn. (Matt. 5:4)
Lord Spirit, give me a horror of sin and deep repentance when I fall. Let me be humble of heart at the least thought of my weakness that I may always be ready to say, "I'm sorry, forgive me."

Blessed those who hunger and thirst for holiness. (see Matt. 5:6)
I have excused myself by thinking holiness is for a chosen few. I am afraid of realizing You desire me to be holy. I must hunger for it before You can feed me with Your grace. I must thirst for it before You can give me living water.

Blessed the merciful. (Matt. 5:7)
I desire everyone to understand my failings, but I tend to be hard and unforgiving with the faults of others. Help me, Jesus,

to be ever ready to forgive so Your mercy will cover over my weaknesses.

Blessed the pure of heart. (Matt. 5:8)
So many desires, goals, and ambitions clutter my mind, dear Jesus. Help me to be single-minded—to desire only You—to work for Your honor and glory—to seek first the Kingdom and to judge everything in the light of Eternity.

Blessed the peacemakers. (Matt. 5:9)
I do not make peace. I am afraid of getting hurt, getting involved. Human respect rules my life, and I prefer to be left alone. My Jesus, the opinions of men meant nothing to You. Help me to make peace, root out discord, and sow the seeds of unity.

Blessed those who are persecuted in the cause of right. (Matt. 5:10)
I tend to join the crowd, Lord Jesus. Help me to stand alone if necessary and fight for Your Church, Your commands, and Your principles. Let my motto be, "Who is like God?" and my goal, that all men know of Your love and redemption.

Blessed are you when people abuse you and persecute you and speak all kinds of calumny against you for My sake. (Matt. 5:11)
My Lord, I tend to change my opinions, retract my statements and become silent in the midst of the majority. Help me with the gift of Fortitude to form my opinions by Your standards, to bravely state the faith and morals Your Church proclaims, and to resist all forms of permissiveness. Let me be content to know I please You. I pray for all those whose lives are disturbed by their adherence to Your commandments. Give us all perseverance, courage, and strength to withstand the onslaughts of the Enemy and the world.

Our Father, Who Art in Heaven — My Lord and God, I do not appreciate the privilege and dignity You have given me. I use the title Father with a cold heart and blank mind. I have lowered the dignity of being Your child to the level of a pilgrim in a stranger's house. Your paternal love and care seem as far from me as the earth is from the heavens. My ingratitude astounds me, and my lack of comprehension manifests my spiritual immaturity. Forgive me, Father. Give me a childlike confidence, quick recourse to Your protection, and total confidence in Your providence.

Hallowed Be Thy Name — I am afraid, my Lord, that it is my name and my dignity on which I spend much time and concern. I do not take advantage of the many opportunities afforded me every day to glorify Your name. Human respect holds my tongue and suppresses the inspirations Your Spirit gives me to proclaim Your name. Give me the grace to hold the opinions of men as nothing. Do not permit me to be dragged to and fro — constantly changing from one opinion to another in order to please the world. How fruitless is a life spent trying to please the unpleasable.

Thy Kingdom Come — I am negligent in spreading Your Word, Lord Father. My life does not mirror the perfections of Jesus so the world will know He is Lord. I leave to others the obligation of spreading the Good News. Give me a missionary spirit so I may take advantage of every opportunity to save souls. Many souls are lost because no one cares for them or their salvation. Give me energy and love so no obstacle will be too great to overcome in spreading Your Kingdom in men's hearts and in the world.

Thy Will Be Done on Earth As It Is in Heaven —I find Your Will difficult at times, my Lord, and I rebel. I do not make enough effort to discern Your Will; neither do I judge my life or decisions by the rod of the Gospel. I find excuses in not accomplishing Your Will—excuses that are designed to deaden my conscience, but deep in my soul, I know I do my own will. Never permit me to smother my conscience so I am blind to Your Will! Help me, forgive me, and give me strength to prefer You to myself.

Give Us This Day Our Daily Bread —I am not always grateful, my Father. My pride makes me think I am providing everything that is necessary for life. Give me a spirit of humility and dependence. Let me look to You for everything I need in body and soul. Purify my soul so I may receive the Eucharist worthily. Humble my heart so I may be grateful for Your Providence and ever trust Your Wisdom.

Forgive Us Our Trespasses, as We Forgive Those Who Trespass Against Us, and Lead Us Not into Temptation, But Deliver Us from Evil —Lord, have mercy on me! In this petition I ask that You forgive me in the same way I forgive others. When forgiving others is hard, bring this petition to my mind so I may forgive with a loving heart.

Help my weaknesses and give me the strength not to put myself in circumstances that may lead me to offend You. Do not permit me to overlook or omit good works because of laziness or human respect. Do not let me enter Eternity to see what I might have been, but let me correspond to every light, every grace, every inspiration.

Precious Blood of Jesus, purify my soul, make my conscience sensitive to sin, make my heart humble and docile, and wash away all my sins and faults. Present me one day to Your Father as a perfect image of You!

STRUGGLE OF A SOUL'S PURIFICATION

Lord Father, do not put my soul to the test. I am beset with temptations of every kind. Invisible forces crowd in upon me, and I cannot see Your Face. The Presence that gave me courage in trials, peace in turmoil, and strength in difficulties has all but disappeared from view. I call and You do not answer, I seek and do not find, I search but to no avail. I seem to catch a glimpse of You at times, but it is only a memory of the past. I see nothing but myself in the depths of my being. I see only the evil person that I am capable of being. I see my soul as three rooms. One room is called Memory, one Intellect, and one Will. There are times, my Father, I am locked in the room—Memory. All is dark and filled with the ugly presence of the real me. At times it is like a room without an exit, and then the least sign of love from my neighbor—a smile, a touch, a prayer, suddenly opens a door ever so slightly, and I breathe a sigh of relief. And then the door is closed again, and the struggle goes on. There are times of hope as I somehow escape to the room called Intellect, whose door is never closed. I go in and reason my plight, but I do not seem to be able to stay long. All the methods and arguments I find there to keep that invisible force from destroying me merely confirm what I already know in the depths of my being. I go into that room to find new weapons, but only find the old ones I have been using. My soul is frightened at the prospect of no relief, but then a friend passes by, and again a glance of love and concern calms my soul.

As I walked away from the room called Intellect, I heard a voice say, "Look into the room called Will." I walked inside and the gentle voice of Faith said, "Take me with you—do not fear." I found in that place pure love—strong love—determined love. I found new weapons—Will and Love—the kind of love that is not dependent on feelings—the kind that is consistent, like God's love. Yes, Lord Father, I would like to live in this room—the room of Will and Love.

I stumble into the room almost feebly, and look at the power and Presence within it. It is a paradox—it seems that suddenly the darkness in my memory and the Faith in my intellect join forces and let me stand in the door way of Will. Faith beckons me to do rather than rest in darkness — to accomplish rather than question why — to admit what I am before You, Lord Father, and do Your will with love — to be willing to suffer the vacuum in my soul, the darkness of my mind, the uncertainty of my way and still accomplish Your Will — to say, "I love You" when only the deafening sound of silence rings in my ears — to say, "I believe" when the void before creation calls out to me — to understand that this is for my good when futility surrounds me like a cloak.

Do you hear my sighs of pain as I struggle to rise above the darkness? Yes, I know You do. Does it hurt You to see me struggle and search to be what You want me to be? Will I ever cross that bridge called Humility so I can accept myself and keep my eyes on You? Can I stand before You willing to feel my sinner condition and keep my eyes on Your beauty?

Give me a pure heart and a strong will so my seeking will ever reach out to You as I feel my weaknesses. Strengthen my faith so I will never look for reasons or excuses. Let my hope grow deeper as I realize Your power is working in the darkness of my soul.

There is something deep within me that makes me somehow feel a Presence in the midst of an absence, Your compassionate

Heart in the midst of one so empty, Your merciful glance that somehow wishes things were not so, but knows there is no other way but the cross.

Why do I feel like I'm alone on a desert waste? How is it I know I am so loved by God and yet feel so lonely? What a wretched state to think even for a moment that the knowledge of God's love is not enough. Are you saying, my Father, that my heart is not all empty so You can fill it? Must my walk be in pure faith, my only assurance Your providence and my strength Your Will? Must my soul cry out in anguish and then hear only the sounds of its own echo?

I have come to realize, O God, that You are not my All. I thought my heart was detached from everyone and everything, but the purifying fire of Your Spirit touches my soul, and suddenly I see myself on the bottom rung of the ladder, barely able to climb. I stand before You, Infinite Holiness, wanting to shield my eyes, but not daring, even for a moment, to take them from You. I look at Jesus, who took on my humanity and struggled as I struggle. I know He understands, and yet I feel I have disappointed Him. I want to run, but there is no place to go. I want to be transformed, but my lack of courage keeps me from making that giant step. I say, "Yes, Lord, take all," and fear grips my heart. I say, "No, Lord, I cannot," and disappointment envelops me. Tears flood my eyes, and I am ashamed of my lack of courage. Do You cry in me, with me? I do not want to cry alone.

Why do I feel trapped? I know this will pass. I know Your love never leaves me. I know You see my every action, my thoughts are open to you — and yet I feel as if I were in a battle — a battle of wills. I feel my very weaknesses are somehow tools in my hands to fight the enemy. Where is my weakest point? Is the knowledge of my weaknesses my stumbling block, or am I fighting that knowledge? Perhaps I seek perfection thinking Your love would be a reward. Do I find it difficult to accept the reality that Your love is a gift to me, a sinner? You love because you are so good and I am a bungling child, stumbling along each day. Why do I find it so hard to face myself and plunge myself into Your mercy and love? Why can't I honestly present myself before You and drink in Your love? Would this be humility? Am I running from a secret weapon to fight the enemy?

I used to think humility was a matter of humiliations, but, Lord Father, is there any humiliation comparable to the reality of seeing my true self and how I stand before you? Will

I ever accept myself and then be free to try to be like You? Will I ever be able to feel my sinner condition, expect Your power, and then plunge into the ocean of Your mercy? My self-knowledge is no surprise to You, Lord Father. My soul is distressed because my new realization as to the depth of my degradation has made me aware of my need of Your love and Presence while I feel almost pushed away from Your sight. It is as if Your Eyes were cast down at the sight of me. As each new day begins, it seems the distance is further away, and as my soul cries out, "I love You," the echo of my own voice returns and my heart sinks once more into another depth of anguish. I shall wait in hope for Your Eyes to turn toward me. Does it hurt You to wait for the fire to accomplish its work in me? Does Your Heart throb as You hear my voice cry out, "Oh God, lift Your Eyes and look at me — look upon this empty vessel — fill me with Your love — touch me — heal me — chastise me, but never leave me"?

I see Your image reflected in my neighbor, in nature, in events, and my soul is thrilled at the sight, but when I look for more traces of Your Presence, You are gone. My soul becomes restless and tosses to and fro as a child with a high fever. I thirst, and a little Living Water only increases my thirst. It brings back the memory of those times we were at home together, content in each other's Presence. Those days seem so long ago. My heart is consoled at the realization that You knew me then as I know myself now and still You love me. I must wait with patience for Your good pleasure.

Thank you, Father, my soul somehow feels as if a door is opening. It is like hearing a familiar footstep and waiting for the key in the lock that will open the door to a loved one. The room of Memory is still dark and troublesome and little things seem to stir it up easily. As I seek You, even though my soul is in darkness, I feel Your Eyes are no longer cast down. Are You glancing at me? How powerful You are, Lord God, for Your slightest glance brings peace in the midst of turmoil. I seem not to fear the darkness. Have I begun to look at myself without surprise and perhaps accepted my weaknesses? Will I be able to keep my glance ever on You?

If I keep looking at myself I will be facing raw truth, and that sight keeps me in a state of unmitigated turmoil. Help me to be able to feel my weaknesses but keep my eyes on Your beauty and power. This would be freedom—the ability to accept human truth and keep my eyes on Divine Truth—to possess knowledge of my natural worth without losing sight of my supernatural worth—to understand I am capable of any evil, but fully aware that Your grace is at its best in my weakness—to have a consciousness of the possibility of falling, while resting secure in Your mercy—to feel the icy chill of separation while ever resting in Your Love—to see as I am seen and not flinch at the sight, but see the glorious goodness of God as You accomplish a holy work in an imperfect being.

Can I be like Jesus when I find it so difficult to be kind, patient, and understanding? My soul is constantly plunged into darkness, and the tiny glimpse I may have had of You only makes the darkness more black when You are gone. My soul is like a rudderless boat bounced back and forth by the flesh, the world, and the Enemy. Just when I think I have conquered all three, I suddenly find myself bound up in one of them.

Why are there three sources of temptation? Are the temptations of the flesh in the faculty made to Your Image, Father—the Memory? Are the temptations of the world in the faculty made to the Image of the Eternal Word—the Intellect? Are the temptations of the Enemy geared toward the faculty made to the Image of the Spirit—the Will? There is within my soul a battle on three sides. I cry out to You for help, my

Jesus, and I do not hear Your voice. There are times the battle is so fierce I question Your power and my endurance. Forgive me—I seek only Your Will and the glory of Your name.

It seems that the Seven Capital sins often take up residence in a particular faculty. Does God permit this to enable me to make right choices—to confound the Tempter—to utilize grace, to witness to His Power?

It seems as if Lust, Gluttony, and Sloth, the tempters of the Flesh, try to influence the Memory and Imagination. Covetousness and Envy are used by the World to influence the Intellect—while the Enemy desperately tries to acquire the Will by Pride and Anger.

What do I possess, Lord Jesus, to fight such foes? Yes, I possess Your Spirit, Your grace, Your Cross, Your presence, Your love. You have asked me to be merciful and compassionate and to recall the words of Scripture and to pray so that I am not put to the test. And yet, with all these, my Lord, I seem hopelessly entangled in a maze of darkness. What is the shield to fight such powerful foes? Am I to be passive and let the storm rage as I live in Your Presence? Am I to fight the battle of Wills as St. Michael did long ago? Am I to love more when I feel hatred—to be more gentle when anger takes hold of me?

My Lord and Father, I have tried them all, and each in turn gave me an oasis on which to live for a while—a breath of fresh air to revive my drooping spirit—a new direction to take—a new plan of attack. Yes, all these ways of fighting the foe have served me long and well.

Is there a new way—a new path for me to tread? Have I perhaps begun and do not see it? Is this a vacuum that comes from an absence or an emptiness that comes from Light—the Light in the darkness—the Light that penetrates my being and makes me see myself as I stand before my Creator? What do I do at such a sight? What does He want me to do?

The love that took upon Itself my sins "prayed the longer in distress, fear and anguish of heart" (Luke 22:44). In the Garden of Gethsemane He prayed for three hours and asked His Apostles to pray with Him. The Apostles' prayer was to enable them to keep from falling. Like Jesus they were to pray for God's Will and the courage to endure the suffering that would soon befall them.

Jesus was afraid, but He took His distress to His Father. He asked for some other way, but there was none. Suffering was necessary to manifest His love for me. Communion with the Father in prayer kept Jesus in union with the Father's Will.

No matter what the difficulty, Jesus saw the Father's Will and accepted whatever that Will permitted in His life. I am more like the Apostles, who slept, as St. Luke tells us, from "sheer grief" as Jesus agonized in the Garden.

Obviously, prayer did not take away the terrible suffering that was in store for Jesus and His Apostles. What then was the "test" they were asked not to be put through? The test certainly was the way they endured that suffering. I see in the Gospel that Jesus prayed and received strength to face the trials ahead with courage. Humility enabled Jesus to submit to the Father's Will in everything.

The Apostles' pride did not permit them to face reality, so grief took possession of them instead of holy fear and prayer. As a result, the situation forced them to act on an emotional, selfish level, and they could not see the Father's Will. They ran away from the situation first by sleep, then by abandoning Jesus. They did not realize that in proportion as they ran and hid, in that proportion they were miserable. Had they prayed, they would have had the courage to stand by Jesus as His Mother Mary did. I can be reasonably sure that she prayed constantly to the Father for strength to endure the sufferings of Jesus.

Yes, my Father, I pray for the cross to be taken away, for I do not possess the humility necessary to say, "Thy Will be done — not mine." I do not pray "earnestly and longer" — I do not place my soul in darkness and temptation before You and depend upon You entirely.

Lord Father, take my feelings, my anxieties, my fears and weaknesses — they are the only things that are mine to give — take my will and unite it to Yours. Let my strength be in a humble acceptance of myself and my hope be steadfast in Your Will. Let our hearts — Yours and mine — be united in pain, that I may comfort my neighbor in his sorrow. Let our love be one love, that my love for my neighbor may be unselfish.

Oh, God, let the dark night within me unite itself to the Agony of Jesus in the Garden that those who walk in darkness may one day see the Light of the world, for with the dawn comes rejoicing. Truly, there is a quiet awareness of Your Presence in this darkness and anguish. Though I look and do not find, there is a nearness of Love Itself that brings upon me a quiet calm. I push forward to live on a Will level and find myself more patient with my neighbor because I am more aware of my own struggles.

I find myself more capable of loving my neighbor. It is as if the faults that made him difficult to love at times are nothing anymore. The reality of my own weaknesses — weaknesses that are so present and so clear to me — makes me look upon everyone else with greater love. They suddenly seem so much better than I — so much more deserving of love than I. This darkness in my soul makes me love all mankind with a compassionate and unselfish love. Through the maze of their sins and faults I am able to see Jesus. Since I am so full of weaknesses, their weaknesses are no longer an obstacle to my love.

I am free to love and to understand. The spiritual numbness that sometimes accompanies the darkness makes me listen to others. The false concepts of my own strength that made me unable to stop and listen to my neighbor, has been lessened. I am happy with their questions and the opportunity to be of service. The darkness in my soul sees only other souls also struggling, also in anxiety of heart.

The purifying flame of Your Spirit that touched my soul and plunged it into agony, forced it to rise above itself. Prayer is no longer a time of conversation with God but a deep awareness of Holiness Itself — ever present — ever merciful — ever loving — ever awesome. The weaknesses in me see the agonies of Jesus as He lived on earth and the tender justice of the Father. It is as if I am all sin, gazing at infinite holiness. It is frightening and yet without fear. His love for me seems so much more important than my love for Him. He is all and I am nothing.

The struggles and darkness that force me to live on a Will level make me seek God's Will as a welcome haven of rest. My sinner condition makes me want to do His Will over my own. I am no longer sure of my will since the real me is ever present before me. Now I see the wisdom in His Will, His timing, His designs. I watch Him evolve events, and then I step into them with confidence, for He alone is my security. Whatever happens in my moment-to-moment living, I am only to make myself available to its demands without worry, for He alone bears fruit.

What a paradox! "Unless a grain of wheat falls into the ground and dies it remains alone" (John 12:24). My refusal to face myself keeps me from "falling into the ground" and prevents me from dying to myself, but His Love plunges me headlong into the ground of self-knowledge, and in the darkness of humility the seed of my soul grows into a tree—a tree that is beginning to bear the sweet blossoms of His fruit.

How great You are, O God, for You still call out to the void — to the darkness — to nothingness and say "Let there be light."

Mother M. Angelica
(1923–2016)

Mother Mary Angelica of the Annunciation was born Rita Antoinette Rizzo on April 20, 1923, in Canton, Ohio. After a difficult childhood, a healing of her recurring stomach ailment led the young Rita on a process of discernment that ended in the Poor Clares of Perpetual Adoration in Cleveland.

Thirteen years later, in 1956, Sister Angelica promised the Lord as she awaited spinal surgery that, if He would permit her to walk again, she would build Him a monastery in the South. In Irondale, Alabama, Mother Angelica's vision took form. Her distinctive approach to teaching the Faith led to parish talks, then pamphlets and books, then radio and television opportunities.

By 1980 the Sisters had converted a garage at the monastery into a rudimentary television studio. EWTN was born. Mother Angelica has been a constant presence on television in the United States and around the world for more than thirty-five years. Innumerable conversions to the Catholic Faith have been attributed to her unique gift for presenting the gospel: joyful but resolute, calming but bracing.

Mother Angelica spent the last years of her life cloistered in the second monastery she founded: Our Lady of the Angels in Hanceville, Alabama, where she and her Nuns dedicated themselves to prayer and adoration of Our Lord in the Most Blessed Sacrament.

6/9/2017